WAR SCARE ON THE RIO GRANDE

In appreciation of **Mrs. Margaret McAllen** *and* **Mrs. Betty Murray.**
To honor their leadership and generous support of education and the preservation
and study of history in South Texas and the Lower Rio Grande Valley of Texas and Mexico,
The Texas State Historical Association acknowledges that publication of this book
has been partially underwritten by generous gifts from:

Mr. and Mrs. Orvis Akers
Mrs. Lucile Allen
Atlas & Hall
Gillespie Baker
Mr. and Mrs. Joe Charles Ballenger
Steve Bentsen
Jim Tom Boone
Juan R. Brittingham
Daniel Yturria Butler
Mrs. Lydia Yturria Butler
Mrs. H. E. Butt
Mr. and Mrs. Joe Chapa, Jr.
James H. Clement
Mr. and Mrs. George O. Coalson
Stella C. Cole

Mr. and Mrs. Charles A. Colhoun, Jr.
Shelley H. Collier, Jr.
Mr. and Mrs. Robert Compere
Mrs. C. M. Cozad
James L. Donnell
Ralph Durden
First Bank
Mr. and Mrs. F. A. Garza, Jr.
Congressman Kika De La Garza
Mr. and Mrs. W. P. Glass
Robert L. Gray
Mr. and Mrs. John W. Griffin
Mr. and Mrs. Dave Grosz
Harlingen National Bank
Mr. and Mrs. Edward H. Harte

Ms. Virginia M. Hartnell
Byron Howard, M.D.
Mr. and Mrs. Charles Hubbard
Dr. and Mrs. Philip Hunke
Mr. and Mrs. Glenn Jarvis
Carl H. Judin, Jr.
Keller Texaco Service
Mr. and Mrs. Robert Kelso
Rollins M. Koppel
Henry G. Krausse, Jr.
Kreidler Funeral Home, Inc.
Phil La Mantia
Mr. and Mrs. Argyle A. McAllen
James A. McAllen
McCaleb Funeral Home

Louise Hill McDonald
Mr. and Mrs. Felix Martinez
Mid Valley Bank
Margaret Ramage
Charlie and Billie Rankin
San Benito Bank & Trust Company
Dr. and Mrs. Carl Seale
Joan L. Stanley, Fun-N-Sun
Texas Bank & Trust
Texas Commerce Bank
Texas State Bank
Mr. and Mrs. Henry B. Webb

Frank N. Samponaro & Paul J. Vanderwood

War Scare on the Rio Grande

Robert Runyon's Photographs of the Border Conflict, 1913-1916

PUBLISHED FOR THE BARKER TEXAS HISTORY CENTER BY THE TEXAS STATE HISTORICAL ASSOCIATION

Published for the Barker Texas History Center by the Texas State Historical Association
in cooperation with the Center for Studies in Texas History at the University of Texas at Austin

Number One in the Barker Texas History Center Series. Series Editor, Don E. Carleton

Library of Congress Cataloging-in-Publication Data

Samponaro, Frank N., 1940–
    War scare on the Rio Grande: Robert Runyon's photographs of the border conflict, 1913-1916 / by Frank N. Samponaro
    and Paul J. Vanderwood. p. cm.—(Barker Texas History Center series: no. 1) Includes bibliographical references (p.) and
    index. ISBN 0-87611-099-5 (cloth: acid free paper). —ISBN 0-87611-100-2 (limited ed.: acid free paper).
      1. Mexico—Frontier troubles—1910. 2. United States. Army.—History—Punitive Expedition into Mexico. 1916. 3. Mexican-American
Border Region—History. 4. Texas—History—1848-1950. 5. Mexico—Frontier troubles—1910—Pictorial works. 6. United States. Army—
History—Punitive Expedition into Mexico. 1916—Pictorial works. 7. Mexican-American Border Region—History—Pictorial works.
8. Texas—History—1848-1950—Pictorial works. I. Vanderwood, Paul J. II. Runyon, Robert, 1881-1968. III. Title.
IV. Series: Barker Texas History Center series (Texas State Historical Association): no. 1.
    F391.S225 1991   976.4'4—dc2O   91-8124 CIP

DEDICATED

to our parents, families, and friends

Contents

Foreword

War Scare on the Rio Grande is the first in a series of monographs to be produced as a result of a cooperative publishing effort between the Eugene C. Barker Texas History Center of The University of Texas at Austin and the Texas State Historical Association. A cooperative program between these two organizations is most appropriate. The Center, formerly known as the University Archives, and the Association have had a long and close relationship. Historical materials acquired by the Association were donated to the University Archives beginning in 1911, and the two organizations began sharing quarters in 1945 with the formal establishment of the Barker Center. Today the Center serves as the primary research library and archive for various Association projects, including its Handbook of Texas Project and *Southwestern Historical Quarterly*. In addition, the Association's historically valuable non-current records are housed in the Barker Center.

The Barker Texas History Center Series results from the Center's desire to encourage and support the publication of historical studies based largely on research done in Barker Center collections. The single most important resource in existence for the study of things Texan, the Center's extensive book, manuscript, map, newspaper, sound, and photograph collections make it a treasure trove for the study of Texas and the regions of which it is a part. The Center is a unit of the University's General Libraries and is open to anyone desiring access to its resources.

The Barker Center acquired the bulk of its Robert Runyon Photograph Collection in 1986 through the generosity of Delbert Runyon and Amali Runyon Perkins and the entire Runyon family. The family later donated additional photographs as well as Runyon's personal papers. The Runyon Collection is not the first Runyon gift to come to the University; in 1968, Robert Runyon donated botanical specimens he had gathered during a lifetime of collecting in his beloved Rio Grande Valley. His more than 8,750 specimens are today housed in the University Plant Resource Center.

In 1988 the National Historical Publication and Records Commission (NHPRC) provided funds to the Barker Center to support a project to preserve and to give access to the 14,000 images in the Robert Runyon Photograph Collection. Glass-plate negatives were sleeved, nitrate negatives were duplicated onto safety-base film, and the collection's prints, postcards, and lantern slides were arranged and housed in protective boxes. The collection's 12,595 unique images were reproduced on microfiche, and a guide to the collection was published by the University's General Libraries. In addition, a full description of the collection was entered into national bibliographic data bases. As a result of these efforts the Robert Runyon Photograph Collection is now widely available as a source for the study of the Lower Rio Grande Valley and Northeastern Mexico during the 1910s and 1920s. The collection offers a large and diverse group of images —images that richly document the history of a key borderland region during the first two decades of the twentieth century.

I would like to thank the following people for their contributions in preserving the Robert Runyon Photograph Collection: Denise Joseph, Katherine Adams, Lawrence Landis, Claire Maxwell, Nancy

Taylor, Dorothy Castanon, Carol Williams, Alison Beck, John Slate, Tom Kreneck, Sue Phillips, Carolyn Bucknall, and Harold Billings. Funds from the J.R. Parten Chair in the Archives of American History provided partial support for the preparation of *War Scare on the Rio Grande.* My thanks also to Ron Tyler, director of the Texas State Historical Association, and to the Association's Executive Council for its crucial support and cooperation. George Ward, assistant direc- tor of the Association, has done his usual excellent job in supervising the many details of getting a book in print. I look forward to the publication of other volumes in the Barker Texas History Center Series in the near future.

DON E. CARLETON
Director
Barker Texas History Center

Preface

At the start of the century you could tell good photographers by the stain on their fingernails. If the nails were a healthy dark tan, like those of Robert Runyon, you knew they used pyrogallic acid as a developing agent. Pyrogallic acid caused some unsightly fingernails, but it gave photographs the best black-and-white tones of the times. And Runyon never let personal vanity stand in the way of a good picture.

This was no amateur at work along the Lower Rio Grande. Although entirely self-taught, Runyon was the consummate professional who in the heyday of his photographic work from 1910 to 1926 experimented with the most up-to-date lenses, cameras, and film in order to create the best possible images of the region he so appreciated. Vouchers in his remaining personal papers tell the story: yet another special lens ordered from Germany, as well as a newfangled camera, said to be an improvement over the one received last month from New York, and subscriptions to contemporary photography journals from England such as *Portrait Studio*, *Photography of Today*, *Human Anatomy*, *Photographs for Papers*, *Marvels of Photography*, *Practical Drawing*, *Practice of Oil Painting*, and *Sketch Portraiture*.

Naturally, all of this professional drive cost Runyon a lot of money, and he also had a wife and budding family, which eventually reached six children, to support. So while he ran a photo studio in Brownsville, Texas, he also bought into a curio shop with his brother-in-law across the Rio Grande in neighboring Matamoros, Mexico. And no one ever accused Runyon of not knowing how to make money. Besides the portraits he sold to patrons, he fed pictures of news

events to big city dailies in Houston and San Antonio, Dallas, and even New York; produced thousands and thousands of picture postcards for distribution throughout the country, even internationally; and did photo promotion work for a variety of businesses, like the land colonization companies trying to induce immigration to the Valley. And at his Mexican curio shop, just off the main plaza, he vended everything from fancy French perfumes to postcards of some local scenes.

So Robert Runyon was both artist and entrepreneur. His artistry did not tend toward the surrealism which was starting to inform the artistic mind elsewhere at the time. His was more a romantic realism. He loved, for instance, the soft, human detail of the photographs in *National Geographic*. Most of his work, as seen in the images selected for this book, was much more realistic than impressionistic, although he was not averse to adding a few clouds to blank skies if he thought such "doctoring" would increase sales. Still, Runyon aimed to capture the natural ecology and environment of the Valley on film. No one knew more than Runyon about the plants and wildlife in the region, which encompassed Cameron, Willacy, Hidalgo, and Starr counties in the southmost tip of Texas, and Mexican territory on the south side of the Lower Rio Grande. Robert Runyon earned himself international acclaim studying the region's plant life with some of the best botanists of the day. He wrote books about it and preserved its intricate variety on film for us today.

Only when it came to the river itself did Runyon seem to allow himself some artistic license. The Rio Grande was at that time a truly majestic river, especially in the way that it meandered so freely through its immense delta, extending far above Brownsville and Matamoros, and eventually poured into the Gulf. Of course, it could be a mean river, too, and Runyon had plenty of opportunity to photograph its destructive side. Brownsville is built on the highest ground in the delta but is only thirty feet above sea level. Nonetheless, most times the mighty river served human beings, irrigating their farms and providing major transport for the region. He saw the river as life-giving. Both above and below it lay desert, but along it prospered a unique ecological realm. Runyon felt the need to preserve that peculiar environment so that it would never be lost to memory, and he did so with his camera. The river in all its grandeur and mystery simply enveloped Robert Runyon.

Perhaps more so because Runyon came from big-river country. He had been born along the great Ohio River and only after a basic schooling and a series of minor jobs in the North did he venture to Houston for work that soon took him to the Lower Rio Grande. He arrived in Brownsville in 1909, an enterprising man of twenty-eight, and shortly thereafter married Amelia Medrano Longoria, a young lady from a well-known, old Mexican family, and settled into his photography work.

Soon business was booming, for in 1910 revolution erupted in Mexico, tossing the border region into turmoil. Runyon supplied newspapers anxious for pictures of the momentous events unfolding along the Rio Grande. As the rebellion just happened to coincide with the Golden Age of the picture postcard, Runyon also delved deeply into that market. Following an initial overview of Runyon's life and work, this book provides the historical context for three events that highlighted those tumultuous times which Runyon photographed: the agrarian reform program launched by Mexican colonel Lucio Blanco outside Matamoros in 1913; the border raiding that climaxed in the U.S. side of the Valley in 1915; and the mobilization of U.S. troops around Brownsville in 1916.

As a resident of the region, Runyon naturally knew the territory and had the personal contacts where these happenings took place. He also had good fortune. A Mexican relative of his wife joined the revolution as it approached Matamoros and soon was close enough to the movement's leader, Lucio Blanco, to recommend a local photographer to record his accomplishments. That is how Robert Runyon got his historic shots of Blanco's land reform program.

Throughout the political changes that wracked Mexico during this period Runyon seemed to remain the neutral observer. He photographed stalwarts of the Porfirian dictatorship as easily as the rebels who overthrew it. In fact, his son Delbert believes that his father probably endorsed Don Porfirio, except for the corruption in his dictatorship. And a daughter, Amali Runyon Perkins, confirms her father's insistence on orderly government on both sides of the border. Moreover, as an unwavering liberal Southern Democrat who in the early 1940s became Brownsville's mayor on a reform ticket which labeled him a kind of "populist," Runyon probably did not appreciate Blanco's confiscation and subsequent division of private property. Amali agrees that her father was a stickler for judicial procedure and the protection of people's rights.

Whatever his political bent toward the happenings he photographed, Runyon possessed a solid sense of history; that is, he had a genuine appreciation for the past. His large library was well stocked with history books, and he owned an especially impressive collection of volumes about the Mexican War. Runyon told his children that he collected and saved items from the past, even his own personal effects, so that they would understand the links between past and present. And the lesson obviously took—thank goodness that it did—because it led the children to preserve their father's photographs, glass negatives, photo equipment, and personal correspondence, which they later donated to the Barker Texas History Center at the University of Texas at Austin.

The important Robert Runyon collection of 12,595 unique photographic images, plus the prints and correspondence, have been meticulously copied, catalogued, and preserved at the Barker Center. Although the collection runs from 1910 to 1947, most of the photographs are concentrated in the period from 1910 to 1926, which is the focus of this book. Unfortunately, thousands of celluloid negatives have already been lost to the heat and humidity of the Lower Rio

Grande, but plenty remain, and they have been carefully cleaned and placed in acid-free paper envelopes. Finally, all the negatives have been placed on microfiche, a demanding skill which has yet to be perfected, to ensure the Runyon photographs a wide distribution among universities and libraries, allowing both scholars and amateurs to enjoy, analyze, and utilize the invaluable images. The photographs complement the Barker Center's already strong manuscript holdings on South Texas as well as the incomparable documentation on the Mexican Revolution in the Nettie Lee Benson Latin American Collection at the University of Texas at Austin.

The Barker collection certainly does not contain all of the Runyon photos in existence. Some for this book were found in the archives of historical museums and libraries, others in the personal collections of individuals such as Donald T. Stiff of Longwood, Florida, and Carl T. Marcoux of Irvine, California, whose fathers participated in the border mobilization and collected Runyon photos to remember it. Still others belong to venerable postcard collectors, such as John Hardman of Warren, Ohio, who specializes in cards on the Mexican Revolution. Undoubtedly the net for Runyon photos could have been cast even more widely; they seem to exist everywhere. But this book presents a fair sampling of his work.

Naturally, we received a good deal of help in exploring the life and work of Robert Runyon for this volume. And we mean to thank you all for what has truly been a collaborative endeavor. Nothing could have been accomplished without the steady support of Runyon's children themselves, in particular Delbert Runyon, the youngest son, now teaching school in Brownsville, who vividly remembers working side by side with his dad in the family's photo laboratory and who so willingly told us about it. We also acknowledge a special debt to Amali Runyon Perkins, who provided many documents and details of her father's life and who championed her mother's role in the Runyon partnership. Additional details and insights came from Lillian Runyon Mahoney of Corpus Christi, another Runyon daughter, and William T. Runyon of Fort Worth, a grandson, along with other members of the Runyon clan.

In the search for additional Runyon material we called upon old friends who have helped us in other work with picture postcards, people like John Hardman of Warren, Ohio, who responded with enthusiasm. In the Rio Grande Valley people could not have been more hospitable in opening their photo archives to us: Henry Krausse of the Brownsville Historical Association, David Mycue of the Hidalgo County Historical Society; Brian Robertson of the Brownsville Historical Museum, Yolanda González, chief archivist at the Arnulfo Oliveira Memorial Library in Brownsville, and Bruce Aiken, a specialist on Fort Brown who guided us around the old encampment. The Texas State Historical Association and its director, Ron Tyler, have been most supportive. George Ward, assistant director of the TSHA, supervised the transformation of our manuscript and Robert Runyon's photographs into this book with great skill and efficiency. We appreciate his efforts on our behalf. Particular thanks are due to the Eugene C. Barker Texas History Center at the University of Texas at Austin and its director, Don Carleton, for encouragement and funding. His staff dedicated many hours to this project, which is the first volume in the Barker Texas History Center Series published by the Texas State Historical Association. Lawrence A. Landis and his fine staff in the photographic division of the Barker Texas History Center loaned us their technical expertise with the photographs themselves and taught us to handle them with soft, white cotton gloves, while Ralph Elder patiently steered us through the Runyon papers at the Center. Finally, a special word of thanks is due to the University of Texas of the Permian Basin for financial support that helped make possible the research for this book. We thank you all for your valued contributions.

Robert Runyon in 1938. Courtesy of Amali R. Perkins.

1. Robert Runyon: Border Photographer

"Photo by Runyon, Of Course." Robert Runyon proudly affixed a label with that slogan to the frames of thousands of portraits he made in his Brownsville studio, and as the photographs in this book attest, he was a marvelously talented photographer. His pictures richly document the growth and development of cities and towns in the Lower Rio Grande Valley and the lives of their residents during the second and third decades of the twentieth century. They also provide a unique record of the agriculture and natural plant life of the region during the same period. Runyon's spectacular coverage with his camera of the tumultuous revolution raging in northeastern Mexico in 1913–1914 illuminates critical social and political questions, while his photos of the "bandit" raids in the Brownsville area in 1915 and the buildup of U.S. military forces along the border in 1916 are of great historical value. Even though Runyon's most enduring legacy is his work as a professional photographer, he was an extraordinary individual who distinguished himself in other fields of endeavor as well. His research on the flora of the Lower Valley brought him international recognition, and he earned considerable acclaim as a politician, civic leader, businessman, and author.

Robert Runyon was born on a farm near Catlettsburg in Boyd County, Kentucky, on July 28, 1881, the son of Floyd and Elizabeth (Lawson) Runyon. Like many farm boys of his generation, he received only a limited formal education that did not extend through high school, a handicap he overcame in later life through self-instruction, determination, and sheer natural intelligence. As a young man Runyon left the family farm and went to work as a yard clerk for the Norfolk and Western Railroad in Williamson, West Virginia. It was at this time that he first tested his entrepreneurial and technical skills by publishing a pamphlet explaining how to silverplate mirrors and emboss, etch, and foil glass. The pamphlet cost one dollar postpaid, and for an another ten cents the author promised to provide readers who had questions with additional advice. On September 16, 1901, Runyon married Norah Young in Ironton, Ohio. The couple's only child, William, was born on August 6, 1904, in Ashland, Kentucky, where Runyon had recently taken a job selling insurance. Had not a personal tragedy ensued, Robert Runyon might well have spent the rest of his life in Kentucky with his family. But the death of his wife on December 3, 1908, profoundly affected his future.[1]

In an effort to put the impact of Norah's death behind him, Runyon left William with his late wife's parents and went first to New Orleans and then to Houston to look for work. In early 1909 the Gulf Coast News and Hotel Company hired him to sell sandwiches, fruit, candy, and cigarettes to passengers on the St. Louis, Brownsville, and Mexico Railway between Houston and Brownsville, Texas. Runyon favorably impressed his superiors at the company, and within a couple of months they offered to make him manager of Gulf Coast's lunchroom and curio shop in the Brownsville depot. Runyon, who liked what he had seen of Brownsville during his visits there on the train, accepted. In April 1909 he rented a room for himself across the street from the railroad station and began a period of residency in Brownsville that continued without interruption for fifty-nine years until his death in 1968.[2]

When Runyon moved to Brownsville, it was a city of about 10,000 and the site of a deactivated army post, Fort Brown.[3] Situated across the Rio Grande from Matamoros, Tamaulipas, Mexico, it was the seat of Cameron County and the leading financial, agricultural, and wholesale distribution center of the Lower Rio Grande Valley. While the territory encompassing what were then the three counties of the Lower Valley (Cameron, Hidalgo, and Starr) was a fertile delta with rich agricultural potential, that potential until shortly before Runyon's arrival in the area had been largely unrealized because of the remoteness and isolation of the region. Prior to the completion in 1904 of the St. Louis, Brownsville, and Mexico Railway, transportation and communication with major U.S. population centers and markets had been slow and costly. Once a means was established to move farm products quickly and cheaply to northern markets, the systematic exploitation of the agricultural possibilities of the region began, producing an influx of people.[4] Between 1900 and 1910 the population of the Lower Valley increased from 34,401 to 54,037. In 1920 it stood at 85,861 and in 1930 at 176,452.[5]

The expanding economy and growing population of the Brownsville area provided Runyon with an opportunity to supplement the modest salary that he earned as the Gulf Coast News and Hotel Company's local lunchroom manager. It was an opportunity that he eagerly seized. The small curio shop that occupied one corner of the depot lunchroom displayed a number of items for sale to tourists, including inexpensive jewelry, Indian moccasins, Mexican handicrafts, newspapers, and picture postcards.[6] Runyon, who had been an avid amateur photographer since purchasing an inexpensive Kodak 3A camera in 1907, thought that he could make some extra money by selling his customers his own postcards instead of those of other people.[7] He also recognized that before taking this step he had to learn a good deal more about the postcard business. With a thoroughness that characterized his business practices throughout his life, he wrote to several postcard publishers to inquire about the cost of making commercially printed postcards from his photographs.[8] In a typical response to his letters of inquiry, the C. V. Williams Photograph Company of Bloomington, Indiana, whose slogan

One of Robert Runyon's earliest local view postcards shows the St. Louis, Brownsville and Mexico Railway depot in Brownsville, where he managed the lunchroom and curio shop from April 1909 until January 1912. Courtesy of the Barker Texas History Center.

was "An Artistic Local View Card Is in a Class by Itself," offered to furnish him with local view cards made from his photos at six dollars per thousand.[9] By mid-1910 Runyon had a number of photos that he had taken of Brownsville-area scenes made into postcards and was selling them at the depot curio shop. He felt secure enough financially that summer to return briefly to Kentucky to bring his son, William, to Texas to live with him.[10] At the end of November he wrote enthusiastically to an acquaintance from Kentucky about his recent business venture and new place of residence:

. . . I am sending you under separate cover a few local views of Brownsville and a souvenir folder of Brownsville. They are in my own makeup and are original. I made the photographs and had the cards made from them and have many other view subjects in print now.

I was born and raised in Catlettsburg and still love the town, but I am now a citizen of Brownsville, Texas, and could never be induced to return to the east.

We have here the best climate, and the most aggressive small town in the United States.[11]

Robert Runyon entered the postcard business at a time when thousands of others across the United States were doing the same thing. A national craze for postcards made the first decade and a half of the twentieth century the golden age of picture postcards.[12] By 1910 Americans were mailing nearly a billion postcards annually. They used cards to announce a birth or wedding or to invite friends to Sunday dinner. In an era when not many people traveled very far from home and few small-town newspapers carried news photographs, buying a postcard depicting an event of local, national, or even international interest for oneself or to send to a friend was extremely common. The wide availability of inexpensive view cards stimulated interest in collecting as well as mailing them, and as a result, countless individuals got a glimpse of the major happenings of the day and of scenes of faraway places through the albums on their living-room tables. At the same time, innovations in cameras, film, and printing paper made it possible for virtually anyone to go into the business of making and selling what collectors today call real photo or photographic postcards on a shoestring. Such cards could be produced simply and cheaply by printing negatives directly on special photographic paper with postcard formats on their backs.

Many of Runyon's contemporaries in the postcard business, even highly successful ones like Walter H. Horne of El Paso, sold nothing but real photo cards made in their own studios.[13] Runyon's reliance on both real photo and commercially printed cards is indicative of the sophisticated practices that he used throughout his career as a professional photographer. He turned out his own real photo cards of images, such as those of small groups of individuals, that he expected to sell only in limited numbers. On the other hand, he had

views that he anticipated selling in large quantities, like major buildings and other landmarks in Brownsville and Matamoros, made into printed cards in order to maximize his profit from their sale. Many such cards were manufactured in eye-catching color by the postcard publishers who produced them for Runyon.

Soon after Runyon started marketing his own postcards at the curio shop in the railroad station, he began wholesaling them to other postcard dealers as well. He made photographic local view cards in relatively small batches to accommodate the demand of druggists, cigar store owners, and other retailers in Valley villages like Mission, McAllen, Mercedes, and San Benito.[14] Runyon usually came to town and took his own photographs of scenes chosen by his customers, but occasionally he made postcards from a roll of film sent to him by a small-town merchant who asked that he ". . . please develop and make ½ dozen each of the good ones and send back to me."[15] Such customers also purchased many of his general-interest printed cards. The biggest buyers for these cards, however, were the managers of the large Gulf Coast News and Hotel Company curio shops in San Antonio and Houston, who in 1911 alone bought several thousand of his postcards.[16] Views they purchased included the National Cemetery in Brownsville, banana trees, palm trees, yucca plants, and the fighting-cock pit in Matamoros; most popular were the bullfight scenes that he photographed in the *plaza de toros* of Matamoros.[17]

Despite being a relative novice in the postcard business, Runyon soon sold impressive quantities of his cards. Between October 31, 1910, and August 18, 1911, three postcard printers filled his orders for at least 35,000 cards.[18] At the same time, he himself was making and selling substantial numbers of real photo cards.[19] Although demand for his postcards was strong, Runyon suffered from a problem that affects many inexperienced entrepreneurs. He overestimated the demand for his product, bought too many supplies on credit, and began to have difficulty paying his bills. In August 1911 he received a notice from Tom Jones, a Cincinnati, Ohio, postcard publisher, politely requesting that he pay a bill of $45.50 that had been due since May 20.[20] The Curt Teich Company of Chicago was far more

Runyon at the Rabb Ranch southeast of Brownsville (c. 1913). The ranch was renowned for its many fine palmetto palms (the *Sabal texana*), some of which can be seen in the background. Courtesy of the Barker Texas History Center.

blunt when it wrote him in September for a second time about an unpaid balance of $50.20: "We notify you that unless you send us a remittance for this amount by return mail, we will place the [matter] in the hands of our attorney with instructions to force collection."[21] Faced with the possible seizure and sale of some of his photographic equipment to raise money to pay off his debt to Curt Teich, Runyon managed to come up with the sum he owed the postcard publisher within a week, and by the end of the year the company was again filling his postcard orders.[22] Nevertheless, the experience did teach him a lesson; very few similar letters from creditors can be found in his later personal correspondence.

Runyon recognized that his success as a professional photographer required him to diversify his sources of income in order to protect himself from the inevitable fluctuations in the demand for postcards. He had already started to do so in a limited way in the spring of 1911, when he began developing rolls of film sent to him by local amateur photographers.[23] Then in the fall of that year, he contracted with retail merchants in the Brownsville area to process their customers' film.[24] About the same time, he began to supply photographs, including some of the agricultural crops and natural plant life of the area, to land development companies to illustrate the brochures, pamphlets, and magazines they used to interest prospective buyers in their property for sale in the Lower Rio Grande Valley. While Runyon started taking these pictures to earn some extra money, the activity helped to spark his interest in the study of the flora of the region as a hobby.[25]

By late 1911 Runyon was close to making a decision to resign from his position with the Gulf Coast News and Hotel Company to become a full-time photographer.[26] He had already taken a major step in this direction in mid-September, when he spent the substantial sum of fifty-five dollars to buy a Century View camera with a wide-angle lens, an outfit far better suited than the Graflex he already owned to the landscape photography he was doing for the real estate development companies.[27] Then in November he invested three dollars for a one-year subscription to *Popular Photography,* the first of the numerous journals that he purchased regularly during his career as a photographer.[28] The following month he also bought a series of booklets described by their publisher as the complete self-instruction library of practical photography and also ordered from the Office of the Superintendent of Documents in Washington, D.C., a list of all U.S. government publications on photography.[29] Runyon was determined to teach himself as much as possible about the equipment, techniques, and economics of his business.

Runyon resigned as manager of the Gulf Coast Company's lunchroom and curio shop in January 1912 and became a full-time professional photographer.[30] He was eager to be his own boss and had confidence that he could earn enough money in the photography business to support himself and his son, William. Operating out of a small frame building at 1104 Saint Charles Street in downtown Brownsville, he made a living for the next year and a half mainly by marketing reissues of the popular postcard views in his inventory as well as some new ones. He also continued to process film sent to him by amateur photographers and shopkeepers in the area and to make pictures for the land development companies.[31] He was doing the same kinds of routine work that photographers in cities and towns across the United States were doing, no more. Then quite suddenly, the violence and turmoil spawned by the Mexican Revolution on both sides of the Rio Grande presented him the opportunity to take truly arresting photographs of spectacular news events unlike any that he had taken before and in the process to earn considerably more money at his chosen profession.

Over two and a half years passed after the outbreak in late 1910 of open insurrection against the dictatorship of Porfirio Díaz before any major incidents related to the Mexican Revolution occurred in the Brownsville-Matamoros area. There were episodes of relatively minor violence and a few public scares on both sides of the border, but these did not produce the kinds of dramatic scenes that would make particularly newsworthy photographs. Because the uprising in Mexico appeared by 1911 to possess the potential of spilling over the border, the War Department, as a precautionary measure, ordered a troop of U.S. Cavalry to reoccupy Fort Brown, which had been closed since 1906. However, when no threat to the Lower Rio Grande

Valley materialized from the Mexican side of the international line, this small detachment of troops left the area after only a brief stay, and Fort Brown was once again deactivated.[32]

In early 1913 the Mexican Revolution finally began to have a visible impact on Matamoros. On February 16, the local garrison under the command of Major Esteban Ramos renounced its allegiance to Francisco Madero, Mexico's constitutionally elected president, and pronounced in favor of Félix Díaz, nephew of the now-exiled former dictator, who had rebelled in Mexico City. The conspirators took control of Matamoros and deposed civic officials loyal to Madero without firing a shot.[33] In response to reports from the American consul on the scene that Major Ramos was attempting to extort money from U.S. residents of the Mexican border city, local authorities in Brownsville on February 24 urgently requested aid from Governor O. B. Colquitt of Texas. The following day Colquitt ordered a state militia detachment made up of two cavalry troops and two companies of infantry as well as a group of eight Texas Rangers to proceed at once to Brownsville by special train. They arrived on February 26. Meanwhile the War Department reacted to the apparent threat to American interests in Matamoros by dispatching Troop M of the Fourteenth U.S. Cavalry from Laredo, a total of 175 men, to reoccupy Fort Brown.[34] The arrival of these men, the first small contingent of a force that by mid-1916 would total 40,000 regular Army and National Guard troops in the Lower Rio Grande Valley, calmed the anxieties of Americans on both sides of the border, none of whom suffered any depredations at the hands of Major Ramos and the soldiers under his command.

Indeed the garrison of Matamoros, which pledged its loyalty to General Victoriano Huerta, who had come to power in Mexico City in February at the time of the ouster and assassination of Madero, was soon preoccupied by other matters. The usurpation of the presidency by Huerta had provoked rebellion in much of Mexico: Pancho Villa in Chihuahua, Emiliano Zapata in Morelos, and the Constitutionalists under Venustiano Carranza in parts of the northeast. On April 14 word arrived in Matamoros of a battle two days earlier between federal troops from Monterrey and a force under an obscure

Constitutionalist commander named Lucio Blanco near Aldamas, 120 miles to the south.[35] After his victory at Aldamas, Blanco headed toward the border. By May 14 he had advanced to Río Bravo, forty miles from Matamoros. There he told members of the press who had journeyed to his camp that he intended to attack Matamoros but declined to specify the date. When asked to comment about Blanco's remarks, Major Ramos promised to resist, pledging on his honor as a soldier to defend the city until the last man in his command fell.[36] Under these melodramatic circumstances Blanco broke camp at Río Bravo on May 23 and began his final march toward Matamoros. His attack finally came on June 3. By six o'clock on the morning of June 4 the border city was in rebel hands after heavy fighting.[37] Although a wounded Major Ramos and some of his troops managed to flee across the international bridge to safety on the U.S. side, at least three hundred people, including both combatants and innocent civilians, perished during the bloody battle.[38]

Almost immediately after the fighting ceased in Matamoros on June 4, thousands of curious Brownsville residents streamed across the border to get their first look at the victorious Constitutionalist rebels and to gawk at the scenes of death and destruction. The *Brownsville Herald* described the scene this way: "They came in droves, flocks, herds, crowds. Footback, horseback and automobiling."[39] Among those who crossed the border that day was Robert Runyon, naturally with his camera. He spent all day in Matamoros photographing the dead bodies, the damaged and destroyed buildings, and Lucio Blanco's rebel forces. Over the next few days he returned several times to take more pictures, including some of the public executions of captured federals and federal sympathizers and of a funeral pyre of 170 bodies.[40] Graphic scenes of destruction and death sold particularly well, and Runyon marketed many of his most dramatic images to newspapers in Houston and San Antonio over the next two weeks and then in postcard format over the next several years.[41]

While still savoring the early profits from the sale of these photos, Runyon's career as a photojournalist intersected with the activities of Lucio Blanco as a result of very unusual circumstances. On July 31, 1913, Runyon married a young resident of Matamoros after a courtship of nine months.[42] His bride, Amelia Leonor Medrano Longoria, was from a respected middle-class family with deep roots in northern Mexico. Her sister, Leocadia, was married to Francisco González Villarreal, a Mexican citizen who owned a shoe store in Brownsville. Immediately after Lucio Blanco seized control of Matamoros, González sold his store and joined the rebel army without even bothering to tell his wife. While the reasons for his apparently impulsive actions are unknown, it is clear that he was responsible for putting his sister-in-law's new husband in touch with Blanco. Runyon was grateful for the potential opportunity that his introduction to the rebel leader gave him to take more photographs of the kind that he had recently been selling so profitably. For his part Blanco, like many of his fellow Mexican military chieftains, was undoubtedly anxious to find a photographer to publicize his activities and help him attain greater international recognition.[43]

Runyon spent most of July and early August on a honeymoon trip to his native Kentucky with his wife and son. William, who had already become quite fluent in Spanish, acted as interpreter for the couple. While getting acquainted with her in-laws, Amelia learned to prepare many of her husband's favorite Southern dishes, including chicken and dumplings, corn bread, black-eyed peas with salt pork, biscuits, and cornmeal mush. Immediately following his return to Brownsville, Runyon took advantage of his access to Blanco by making a series of photographs of the Constitutionalist commander and his staff at their headquarters in Matamoros. Even though he managed to do a fair business selling these images as postcards and to newspapers, they proved far less profitable than the dramatic photographs that he had taken in June following the battle of Matamoros.[44]

On August 30, however, Runyon's relationship with Lucio Blanco finally paid major dividends. On that date the first significant land reform of the Mexican Revolution occurred at the Los Borregos hacienda, eight miles east of Matamoros. Blanco confiscated the estate, which had been owned by Félix Díaz, and began to redistribute its lands, granting titles of ownership to thirteen local cam-

Robert Runyon and his bride, Amelia Leonor Medrano Longoria, on the patio of the Medrano family residence in Matamoros following their church wedding on July 4, 1913. The day before, the couple had been married in the civil ceremony required by legislation in effect in Mexico since the Reforma of the mid-nineteenth century. Courtesy of Amali R. Perkins.

pesinos. Runyon recognized that an event of great historical importance was taking place and took picture after picture of the former hacienda laborers receiving their certificates of title from Blanco as the military leader's staff benignly looked on.[45] The demand in the United States for the photographs that Runyon took that day was national in scope because of wide public interest in (and in many cases revulsion at) the confiscation of the private property of a rich and powerful individual for the benefit of the deprived masses. Two major newspapers in Texas, the *Houston Post* and the *San Antonio Express,* printed several of the Los Borregos photographs, as did newspapers throughout the United States that subscribed to the news picture service of the Underwood and Underwood Company.[46]

The very good money that he earned selling his land reform series made Runyon eager to continue to exploit his ties through Francisco González Villarreal to the Constitutionalists. In November 1913 his wife's brother-in-law arranged for him to follow forces under the command of General Pablo González to Ciudad Victoria, capital of the state of Tamaulipas, where they attacked the federal garrison of that city. Runyon left Brownsville in a Model T Ford with a local blacksmith and mechanic, who did the driving and kept the car running on the bumpy, rutted, and rock-scattered trails that in many places served as roads in northern Mexico. Runyon and his chauffeur traveled in a small convoy of automobiles loaded with arms for the Constitutionalists under the command of one of Blanco's officers, a Colonel de Cuer. Near Jiménez, ninety-four miles south of Matamoros and thirty-five miles north of Ciudad Victoria, a telegrapher warned de Cuer that federal troops were approaching. He immediately ordered the convoy to retreat to the nearby village of Dolores until the enemy forces left the area. Late that evening one of de Cuer's own sentinels accidentally shot and killed him. The next morning Runyon and his driver started out again for Ciudad Victoria with two Constitutionalists acting as escorts. From time to time the young rebels nervously fired into the brush at a phantom enemy; one even shot the sight off his comrade's rifle.[47]

Runyon finally arrived in Ciudad Victoria just after General González and his troops captured the city. While he was busy taking pictures of the damage caused by the combat, a local storekeeper who was about to be executed by the Constitutionalists as a federal spy begged him to intercede on his behalf. The photographer, who had become fluent in Spanish, successfully did so, and the man's life was spared. By late November Runyon was back in Brownsville with the first pictures taken by any North American photojournalist of the aftermath of the battle of Ciudad Victoria. As a result, major newspapers in Texas, *Leslie's Weekly* magazine, and Underwood and Underwood eagerly purchased his photographs. On the evening of December 1, he showed many of his best images in lantern-slide format to a full house at the Dreamland Theater in Brownsville.[48]

In the wake of his adventure-filled and profitable excursion to Ciudad Victoria, Robert Runyon maintained his contacts with the Constitutionalists in Matamoros and awaited another suitable opportunity to return to Mexico to take battlefield pictures. That opportunity came in April 1914 as forces under the command of Pablo González prepared to attack Monterrey, the largest city in northern Mexico and a major federal garrison. Runyon traveled as far as the Constitutionalist lines on the outskirts of the city by train and horse-drawn wagon. He then accompanied General González and his men into battle on April 24 and recorded on film their final victorious assault against the federal defenders of the city. About a week later he returned to Brownsville with dramatic combat photographs that newspaper readers across the United States soon viewed.[49]

When Runyon arrived back home, he settled down to help his wife raise the first of their five children, Lillian, who had been born in March.[50] This domestic responsibility did not prevent him from taking immediate steps to add many of the images that he had recently made in Mexico to his inventory of printed postcards. At the same time he began the systematic exploitation of a new and lucrative market for his real photo postcards—the soldiers at Fort Brown.

Because of growing concern in the War Department that the violence associated with the Mexican Revolution might seriously threaten the Lower Rio Grande Valley, the number of troops at Fort Brown was gradually increased from the 175 men who garrisoned it when it was reactivated in February 1913 to 1,900 men in early May 1916 on the eve of the first phase of the massive U.S. military buildup on the border.[51] Soon after his return from Mexico in early May 1914, Runyon became a daily visitor to the fort. He sought out small groups of soldiers training during duty hours and relaxing with their buddies during their free time. The soldiers were eager to pose for him, particularly since he promised to return the next morning with their postcards so that they could mail them right off to the folks back home. Repeating this routine day after day, Runyon churned out large numbers of photographic postcards that he sold to the soldiers at a cost of two for five cents. In order to have the postcards ready overnight, he relied on the assistance of his wife Amelia. The Runyons used kerosene heaters during winter months to warm the darkroom to enable them to develop their glass plate negatives and to make prints more efficiently. On the other hand, the summer heat required that they begin work at least by dawn and that the processing solutions be cooled down with ice or chilled water to avoid reticulation (the formation of webs or veins) on the emulsion in the film.[52]

Selling postcards to the troops at Fort Brown began as a very good business for Runyon in 1914 and 1915 and became a bonanza the following year, when his market grew twenty times larger. The general mobilization of the National Guard for duty on the Mexican border ordered by President Woodrow Wilson on June 18, 1916, resulted in the concentration of 40,000 troops, most of them guardsmen, in the Lower Rio Grande Valley by the end of July. Despite competition from other photographers, demand for postcards was so great that Runyon had all the business that he could handle. The boys from northern states were especially fond of buying views of themselves and their buddies to keep as souvenirs and to send to friends and relatives in their hometowns to show them that they were really in faraway Texas and ready for combat with the Mexicans. Runyon was happy to oblige the troops by making literally thousands of photographic postcards for them. Although many of these cards were unimaginatively posed, they were genuinely personal and sold in great quantities.[53] The same men also proved to be insatiable customers for Runyon's printed postcards. He distributed a small brochure describing these postcards when he went to the camps to photograph the soldiers. The brochure announced the availability of views of the Mexican Revolution: "I have been with the Rebels at several battles and have secured some very excellent and remarkable pictures such as piles of dead soldiers executed, the dead burning and many other remarkable pictures." Also advertised were tropical fruit postcards; Mexican bullfight cards; views of American troops on guard duty along the border; and "typical Mexican scenes," including a hungry burro, Mexican Indians, a humble Mexican home, and a Mexican farmer plowing his small plot. Runyon also reproduced an image of revolutionary leader Emiliano Zapata, entitled "Zapata Leader of the Mexican Revolution of the South," which he had pirated from another photographer.[54] These postcards were so popular among the troops that many of them did not wait for Runyon's visits to the military camps to buy them. Instead, they went to his home during off-duty hours to purchase them from Runyon or his wife.[55]

The summer and fall of 1916 was the period of greatest financial success for Runyon during his entire career as a photographer. While he sold huge numbers of real photo and printed postcards to the troops, he carried on as well with his more normal professional activities. Just as before the military buildup on the border, he supplied local view cards to retail merchants in the Lower Rio Grande Valley, processed rolls of film sent to him by local amateur photographers, and took photographs for the land development companies. His business stationery listed his specialties. They included "original" local view cards, bullfight postcards, commercial photographs with the most modern equipment in the Valley, Kodak finishing of high quality at fair prices, enlarging and copying, and lantern slides.[56]

For reasons over which Runyon had absolutely no control, the boom in his sale of postcards began to wane before the end of 1916. By then many of the National Guard units that had been mobilized for service in the Lower Rio Grande Valley had returned home, and most of the rest were about to follow.[57] As a result, his major market

rapidly dried up. Meanwhile, the deepening crisis in U.S. relations with Germany increasingly dominated newspaper headlines. The intense preoccupation of the American people with events in Europe after the formal declaration of war on the Central powers on April 6, 1917, eclipsed public interest in anything having to do with the Mexican Revolution, including postcards. Public demand for Runyon's cards showing scenes of death and destruction on both sides of the border sharply declined. The battles of Matamoros, Ciudad Victoria, and Monterrey back in 1913 and 1914 among Mexicans were now of little interest in comparison to the combat involving Americans actually going on in Europe. Even the famous Runyon postcards which chronicled the aftermath of "bandit" raids in the Lower Rio Grande Valley that resulted in the loss of American lives as recently as 1915 no longer seemed nearly so immediate or important.[58] Moreover, although instances of violence along the border related to the revolution in Mexico had not completely ceased, they had become less frequent and resulted in the destruction of far less life and property. All of these factors combined by the spring of 1917 to end the visually most dramatic and financially most profitable phase of Robert Runyon's career as a professional photographer.

Faced with a sharp decline in sales of both his real photo and printed postcards, Runyon sought to support his growing family, which by September 1917 totaled four children, by concentrating once again on the more traditional kinds of photography that he had done almost exclusively until the spring of 1913. He renewed his efforts to sell local view cards of Valley towns on both a wholesale and retail basis. He now had his own Model T Ford, purchased in 1915 with some of the early profits of his postcard sales at Fort Brown, making it easier for him to travel to towns in the area to take pictures and to market his postcards. He also continued to take photographs for the land development companies and to process the film of amateur photographers. At the same time, he prepared lantern slides for merchants who wanted to advertise in local moving-picture theaters.[59] In earlier days he had made a fair living doing these kinds of work, but that was no longer possible. Not only did he now have a large family to support, he also had to compete with other established photographers, including some of his own former employees who had left him to go out on their own.[60] Under these circumstances Runyon felt obliged to make a fundamental change in the way that he operated his photo business. In late 1917 he opened a studio to do portrait photography on his property at 1104 Saint Charles Street.[61] He had previously resisted taking this step because he preferred to work outside and because he regarded studio photography with its inevitable schedule of appointments for customers as too confining. Now in the face of financial necessity, he began a new and, from his own point of view, less enjoyable phase of his career and started to acquire the specialized equipment that formal portrait photography required.[62]

Runyon opened his photography studio at 1104 Saint Charles Street in downtown Brownsville in 1917 and operated it until 1926. The building, seen from the southeast side, had a private office for Runyon, a reception area for his customers, a darkroom, and the studio where he took portrait photographs. The latter room was illuminated by natural light filtered through a ground glass skylight (not visible) on the northwest side of the building. After 1926 Runyon continued to use the structure as an office and to house his herbarium. Courtesy of the Barker Texas History Center.

Runyon applied his formidable talent and experience as a photographer to his new area of specialization and quickly earned a reputation as the finest studio photographer in Brownsville.[63] Although there were fewer troops at Fort Brown in late 1917 than a year earlier, he used his contacts to spread the word that he was available to do formal portraits of the officers and enlisted men. In 1918 he became the official photographer for the Brownsville High School yearbook, the *Palmetto*, a function he performed until 1926. In this role he took pictures of high school teams and extracurricular organizations as well as portraits of the seniors.[64] During the same period thousands of local residents of all ages had their photographs made in his studio, at times to mark special moments in their lives such as baptisms, first communions, weddings, birthdays, anniversaries, promotions, and retirements, but often simply because they wanted a professional picture of themselves and their families.

In the decade after he opened his studio, Robert Runyon was in most respects a typical professional photographer who did the same kinds of work as his counterparts in cities and towns throughout the United States. His portraits, postcards, lantern slides, film processing for amateurs and local retail merchants, and pictures for real estate development companies were his bread and butter, a dependable source of income.[65] From time to time, however, his fine reputation led to special requests for photographs. For example, when President-elect Warren Harding visited Brownsville in November 1920 to spend a week hunting, fishing, and golfing, several major news organizations—including the *Chicago Daily News*, the *Dallas Morning News*, the *Houston Chronicle*, the *New York Times*, Underwood and Underwood, and the Central News Photo Service—telegraphed Runyon. They requested that he send them photos of Harding on approval and promised to pay for each one actually used.[66] Runyon complied and received fifteen dollars from Underwood and Underwood for three of his photos, five dollars each from the *New York Times* and the *Houston Chronicle* for one picture of Harding, and three dollars from the *Dallas Morning News* for two photos.[67] In the early and mid-1920s, Runyon periodically supplied pictures to newspapers and magazines in Texas to accompany their feature articles on the

Lower Rio Grande Valley, which was undergoing rapid agricultural development.[68] In one of his more unusual transactions, he signed an agreement with the U.S. Immigration Service to supply its Brownsville office during the fiscal year beginning July 1, 1923, "... with photographic prints of such Chinese or other aliens detained by the Immigration Service, as they might specify, to be used for identification purposes . . ." The price agreed upon was seventy-five cents for each dozen prints.[69]

Runyon's daily routine as a photographer was frequently a hectic one, and Amelia, a wise and devoted wife and mother, intervened whenever she thought it was necessary to shield her husband from the children, who by 1920 numbered three girls and two boys, to give him the time that he wanted to do his work and to pursue his growing interest in botany as a hobby. She gently admonished the children not to bother their father when he was busy.[70] As a result, Runyon managed to get his work done and spend time at his hobby while continuing his practice of buying and conscientiously reading a long list of professional journals to keep abreast of the technological innovations in his profession. His cameras, lenses, darkroom materials, and studio facilities were uniformly of high quality, and his claim on his business stationery that he had the most up-to-date equipment in the Rio Grande Valley was no idle boast.[71]

Still, despite being a talented, hard-working photographer with unusual entrepreneurial skills, economic considerations eventually led him to cease operating his studio at 1104 Saint Charles Street. At a time when increasingly stiff local competition convinced him that he could no longer make an adequate living in his old line of work, he saw the opportunity for a lucrative new commercial venture.[72] Runyon's decision to try to lease his studio to another photographer in 1926 coincided with the birth of his son Delbert, the youngest of his six children. Runyon's new business was a shop that catered to tourists in Matamoros. By 1925 he and his brother-in-law,

Runyon carefully positioned reflectors like the one seen in this test exposure so that the light would be just right for his portrait photographs. Courtesy of the Barker Texas History Center.

Robert Runyon (c. 1918) with his cactus plant collection in the backyard of his home next to his studio at 1104 Saint Charles Street. Delbert Runyon says that his father was a "born collector." With varying degrees of seriousness he collected sea shells, coins, books on botany and history, Indian artifacts, and plant specimens for his herbarium. He never enjoyed dancing, going to the movies, listening to the radio, or, in his later years, watching television. Instead, he was absorbed in his collections and particularly in his study of botany and genealogy until the end of his life. Courtesy of the Barker Texas History Center.

José Medrano Longoria, had become co-owners of a curio store facing the Plaza de Armas, the main square in the center of the city, in a building rented from his wife's brother-in-law, General Francisco González Villarreal, the same man who in 1913 had put him in touch with Lucio Blanco. By 1926 the shop was sufficiently profitable to allow Runyon to close his portrait studio in order to devote more time to its management.

Crucial to the rapid success of the curio store, which was called the Basket Place, was its location. It faced a corner of the Plaza de Armas and was between two large and well-known bar-restaurants, the United States Bar and the Texas Bar, both of which catered to thirsty Americans during prohibition.[73] Besides selling a full line of Mexican curios, the Basket Place offered visiting Americans Robert Runyon's postcards, and the tourists bought them in extremely large numbers primarily because Runyon, in a stroke of inspired marketing, made it so inviting for them to do so. Next to his postcard display racks he placed a writing table and chairs. Runyon provided pen and ink free of charge and sold Mexican postage stamps. There was even a mailbox in the shop from which Mexican postal workers made daily collections. Countless tourists bought and mailed postcards depicting the International Bridge over the Rio Grande, the Matamoros Cathedral, or perhaps a bullfight to friends and relatives on the other side of the border.[74]

Runyon's shrewd management turned the Basket Place into a successful business. Within a few years he bought out his brother-in-law's interest in the shop and became its sole owner. Even the onset of the Depression in the United States in 1929 and the repeal of prohibition in 1933 did not end the profitability of his curio store. Ever the resourceful entrepreneur, Runyon found a new device to attract American tourists to his shop: imported French perfume. Since Mexican import duties on French perfume were far less than the corresponding U.S. duties, Runyon could afford to sell the brands that were the most popular in the United States at a fraction of their cost north of the Rio Grande. He advertised his low prices in the Brownsville newspaper and in the tourist-information brochures that Brownsville hotels provided for their guests. The result was a steady stream of customers from the U.S. side of the border to his shop. Some were weekend visitors from San Antonio and Houston who journeyed to Brownsville on the railroad. Others were so-called home seekers, residents of northern states who were lured to the Valley on excursions sponsored by the land development companies. While these tourists came to the Basket Place primarily to purchase Runyon's French perfumes and Mexican curios, few left his store without buying and mailing at least one of his postcards. The shop facing the Plaza de Armas remained profitable and Runyon's main source of income through late 1937, when he turned over its management to his wife and daughter Lillian in order to devote full time to his new position as city manager of Brownsville. The Runyon women ran the Basket Place until 1939 before selling it to one of their Mexican employees. Until then the shop continued to be the principal outlet for Runyon's printed postcards.[75]

While Runyon marketed the great majority of his postcards in the period from 1926 to 1939 at the Basket Place, he sold additional ones to the owners of other curio shops in Matamoros and a few more at a small gift shop that he owned in Brownsville. All during these years he continued to supply local view cards in real photo format to several merchants in towns in the Lower Rio Grande Valley. In doing so, he adhered to his usual practice of periodically traveling about the area to take pictures so that he could make new cards for these customers.[76] Thus, even though Runyon stopped operating his studio in 1926 and his subsequent efforts to lease it to another photographer proved financially unsuccessful, he did some work as a professional photographer and remained in the postcard business through 1939.[77] By the following year, however, the Basket Place had been sold and Runyon had become increasingly absorbed in Brownsville politics. In March 1940 he took a step that symbolized the conclusion of his career in photography. He contacted the Curt Teich Company, which had supplied him with printed postcards since 1911, and instructed the Chicago concern to destroy all of the plates which had been used to make his postcards.[78] During the rest of his life he took many pictures of the flora of the Brownsville area in conjunction with his study of botany as a hobby, but he never worked as a professional photographer again.[79]

Runyon's insistence that the plates from which his postcards had been lithographed be destroyed is indicative of efforts that began in his earliest days as a postcard photographer to prevent the unauthorized use of his images. Pirating was very common among the freewheeling individuals who made real photo postcards and was virtually impossible to prevent. A photographer merely made a copy negative of the postcard image that he wanted to pirate and printed

cards from it. Nevertheless, Runyon developed unusually strong feelings about the matter. In June 1910 he corresponded with Tom Jones, the Cincinnati postcard publisher who made some of his first printed postcards, to ask his opinion about the desirability of copyrighting his images. Jones urged him not to do so, reasoning that ". . .I do not think it would pay to have these photographs copyrighted. It would cost $1.00 each and, as I will not make these cards for others, it will not be necessary to have them copyrighted on my account. Of course, if anyone else wishes to make these cards, they can do

Faced with increasingly stiff competition from other local photographers by the fall of 1921, Runyon advertised regularly in the *Brownsville Herald*. Courtesy of the Barker Texas History Center.

Robert Runyon (right) and his brother-in-law and business partner, José Medrano Longoria (center), hunting in Tamaulipas near Matamoros, c. 1928. Medrano's servant is also visible in the picture. Courtesy of the Barker Texas History Center.

so and can copy from the post cards we make, but they would not get as good results as they would from the original photograph."[80] Runyon chose not to take this advice and copyrighted the photographs that he sent to Jones to make a series of view cards of the Brownsville area.[81]

By no means did Robert Runyon have all or even most of his photographs copyrighted. He did, however, copyright images that he considered particularly valuable or that he suspected were likely to be pirated. The procedure for obtaining a copyright was quite simple as spelled out in the relevant federal legislation, the Copyright Act of March 4, 1909. The first step was to publish the image in question with the statutory notice of copyright claim inscribed. The notice for photographs and postcards had to contain the word copyright or the letter C enclosed in a circle, accompanied by the name of the copyright owner. Promptly after publication, the copyright claim had to be registered by sending two copies of the photograph or postcard to the Copyright Office of the Library of Congress together with a completed application form and the registration fee, a money order for one dollar.[82] Over the years Runyon repeatedly complied with these instructions to protect what he considered to be important personal property.[83]

Nevertheless, his postcards were occasionally pirated by other postcard photographers, and over the years he himself engaged in the practice in at least a few instances.[84] An important distinction apparently developed in his mind between the unauthorized use of uncopyrighted and copyrighted images. The first he eventually seemed to accept as an unavoidable part of the fiercely competitive postcard business. The second he regarded as absolutely intolerable.

Runyon's dogged determination to protect his copyrighted photographs from use without his permission resulted in an extremely bitter lawsuit against the City of Brownsville. He claimed that in late 1926 he had lent the Chamber of Commerce, an agency of the city, a large number of his copyrighted photographs of Brownsville at the request of the Chamber's director. Runyon contended that the director explained that the photographs would be put into an album that was strictly for his personal office use. Soon thereafter, Runyon asserted that he was surprised and shocked to discover the appearance of many of these photographs in booklets that the Chamber of Commerce published for public relations purposes. Despite his repeated written requests, city officials refused to accept his claims of copyright protection for his photographs or to pay him any money for their use.[85]

Outraged and bitter, Runyon decided in the spring of 1927 to sue the City of Brownsville. He could, however, find no experienced local attorney willing to take on the political establishment and represent him.[86] Therefore, on the recommendation of a friend, in May 1928 he selected Robert E. Cofer, an Austin lawyer, to handle his case.[87] Meanwhile, Runyon made a systematic study of federal copyright law and was soon citing relevant cases to his own attorney.[88]

The case of Robert Runyon versus the City of Brownsville, Texas, went to trial in the federal district court in Brownsville in February 1929. Runyon's lawyer alleged that the Chamber of Commerce had used his copyrighted photographs without his permission and without compensation and that he was entitled to collect damages in accordance with the applicable provisions of federal law. The defense countered that Runyon had agreed to allow the Chamber of Commerce the free use of his photographs and that, consequently, his claim for damages had no merit. The jury never had the opportunity to decide the facts under litigation. Before deliberations began, the defense formally agreed on March 2 to pay him the sum of $4,000 and to pay his attorney's fees and all court costs as well. In return, the City of Brownsville was not required to admit any wrongdoing.[89] Runyon regarded the settlement as vindication for himself personally and a great victory of principle.

When Runyon ran for mayor of Brownsville in 1937, the matter of his litigation against the city eight years earlier became an issue. In response to criticism that his suit had cost local taxpayers thousands of dollars, he replied that he had always permitted public enterprises to use his copyrighted photographs without cost as long as his copyright was respected. The Chamber of Commerce, however, had printed the pictures in question without his permission and

without the copyright notice required on them by law. Since copyrighted property had to be protected from theft like all other property, he argued that he had fought for his rights as a matter of public duty.[90]

Even though Runyon's campaign for mayor in 1937 ended in defeat, members of his ticket, which challenged the entrenched political machine, won control of the city council and engineered his appointment as city manager of Brownsville on December 27, 1937. He served in that position until June 21, 1940. By that date he no longer worked as a professional photographer and his curio shop in Matamoros had been sold. Now increasingly absorbed in politics, he was elected mayor of Brownsville on November 4, 1941.[91] Even after being turned out of office by the voters in 1943, his involvement in politics continued undiminished. He was selected as a delegate in 1944 to the National Democratic Convention in Chicago. After World War II he ran unsuccessfully for the state legislature and then served as chairman of the Cameron County Democratic Executive Committee and as a county election clerk, supervisor, and precinct chairman.[92] He also played an important role in civic affairs as Brownsville civilian defense coordinator, chairman of the city parks board, and as a member and later chairman of the Brownsville Planning and Zoning Board.[93]

Robert Runyon's wide-ranging activities also included publishing and the study of genealogy. In the late 1940s he published the *Brownsville News*, a small weekly newspaper, for a short period of time, and his deep interest in his family genealogy led to three publications: *Genealogy of the Descendents of Anthony Lawson of Northumberland, England* (1952); *Runyon Genealogy* (1955), coauthored with his cousin Amos Runyon; and *Supplement to Runyon Genealogy* (1962).[94]

Robert Runyon's principal hobby throughout his nearly half-century of residency in Brownsville was the study of the flora of the region. As he traveled about the Lower Valley in his early days as a photographer, Runyon, a former farm boy with a keen eye for growing things, became increasingly fascinated with the native plant life of the region: the palm trees, the grasses, the flowers, and especially the cacti. He soon became an avid reader of publications on botany, particularly those dealing with the flora of the Lower Rio Grande Valley, and in the process acquired a valuable personal library. On his frequent excursions through the area to take pictures, Runyon began to take along equipment to collect and preserve plant specimens, as well as his camera. In time his herbarium became one of the largest and finest herbaria in Texas and included samples of one genus and fourteen species of previously unknown plants that he himself discovered. Runyon also wrote scholarly works about the flora that he found so absorbing. He was the coauthor with Ellen D. Schulz of *Texas Cacti: A Popular and Scientific Account of the Cacti Native of Texas* (1930) and the author of *Vernacular Names of Plants Indigenous to the Lower Rio Grande Valley* (1947). As a result of these activities, Runyon became internationally recognized as an authority on the botany of the region and was often consulted about his research by prominent botanists from universities in the United States and abroad.[95]

Runyon's passionate interest in the native plant life of the Lower Valley helped make him an environmentalist long before ecological matters became a matter of general public concern. During his tenure as city manager of Brownsville, he was responsible for the creation of two beautiful parks, Lincoln Park and Resaca Park; funds that he applied for and received from the Works Progress Administration were partially responsible for the development of Lincoln Park. In these parks and elsewhere in Brownsville, Runyon planted thousands of native trees, including the stately *Sabal texana* palm, that he grew from seed at his own expense in his backyard. His ecological crusade was not confined to the three years that he served as city manager. Throughout the rest of his life he remained an outspoken champion of projects aimed at the beautification of public places by the planting of native trees and plants, a cause for which he was a tireless advocate during his many years of service on the city parks board.[96]

Robert Runyon died on March 9, 1968, in Brownsville after a short illness at the age of eighty-seven. He was survived by his wife Amelia, six children, and numerous grandchildren.[97] During his long and eventful life he accomplished a good deal more than most people, and his contributions to society continue after his death. His two works on botany are still read today, while his botanical book collection with its many rare volumes has been given to the library of Texas A&I University at Kingsville. Runyon willed his herbarium to the University of Texas at Austin, in part because of his pride in the fact that five of his six children received undergraduate degrees from that institution. Now permanently integrated into the university herbarium, the specimens that Runyon so painstakingly collected and preserved for over half a century are accessible to those engaged in botanical research. Robert Runyon also left an extraordinarily rich visual legacy to posterity in the form of 12,595 unique photographic negatives and prints that farsighted members of his family donated to the Barker Texas History Center at the University of Texas at Austin. Of general public interest because of their themes and quality, these images are of great value to scholars studying the early twentieth-century history of two nations and are, of course, the basis for this book.

Runyon photographed this scene at the *plaza de toros* in Matamoros in 1910. He first sold the image as a real photo postcard at the lunchroom and curio shop he managed in the railroad depot, but because of its popularity he soon had it made into a printed postcard. Even though the bullfight arena in the picture was destroyed during Lucio Blanco's attack on Matamoros in 1913, Runyon marketed the postcard successfully for several years thereafter as part of his bullfight series. Courtesy of the Barker Texas History Center.

HERE IS TO YOU
BANK SALOON
BROWNSVILLE TEX. E.W. HILL.

WHEN IN MATAMOROS
Remember The
AMERICAN BAR COR.
MAIN PLAZA.

Runyon loved the Rio Grande, and over the years he captured its many moods: in flood, bathed in moonlight, at sunrise, and here at sunset. Courtesy of the Barker Texas History Center.

As Lucio Blanco closed in on Matamoros in June 1913 and Major Esteban Ramos, the commander of the federal garrison of the city, prepared to resist his attack, refugees of all social classes fled across the river to safety in Brownsville. While the well-to-do found comfortable lodging in hotels, many ordinary people, including those in this picture, flocked to the Charity House and overwhelmed its limited facilities. Courtesy of the Barker Texas History Center.

Runyon and his chauffeur left Matamoros in November 1913 for Ciudad Victoria in a convoy that included six automobiles loaded with 3,300 rounds of ammunition for Constitutionalist forces under the command of General Pablo González. Courtesy of the Barker Texas History Center.

Although Runyon arrived at Ciudad Victoria too late to photograph the fall of the city to the Constitutionalists, he did provide American newspaper readers with their first look at the aftermath of the battle, including these captured federal cannons. Courtesy of the Barker Texas History Center.

On his way back to Brownsville in late November 1913, Runyon paused in the village of Padilla, twenty miles northeast of Ciudad Victoria, long enough to photograph this humble home (*jacal*) and its residents. He included the image in the series of postcards that he called "Typical Mexican Scenes" and sold in large numbers during the military buildup in the Lower Rio Grande Valley in 1916. This postcard provided many of those who bought or received it with what they uncritically accepted as a "typical" example of how the Mexican people lived. Courtesy of the Barker Texas History Center.

Runyon returned to Mexico in April 1914 to cover the assault of forces under the command of Pablo González on Monterrey. He photographed these troops as they prepared to defend against a possible federal counter-attack along a railroad spur outside of the city. Courtesy of the Barker Texas History Center.

VIEW OF BROWNSVILLE FROM FORT BROWN.

Brownsville in 1913 was a city of slightly more than 10,000 inhabitants. Although the photograph appears to have been taken from a low-flying airplane, Runyon climbed a wireless transmission tower at Fort Brown to get this perspective. When the military buildup took place in 1916, he sold thousands of postcards with this scene to troops eager to show the folks back home what Brownsville looked like. The caption on the card describing the view contributed to its sales potential. Like other photographers of his era, Runyon became adept at using a pen and India ink to write captions backwards on the emulsion side of negatives so that the captions would print properly on positive postcard images. Courtesy of the Barker Texas History Center.

Piperos, c. 1915. These water sellers are in line waiting to fill up at the Brownsville water works on the southwest corner of Washington Square at Eighth and Madison Street. Each vehicle consisted of a used wine cask (*pipa*) fastened to two wagon wheels drawn by a burro or a horse. The cask had an opening on the top so that it could be filled with water from an overhead valve. Water was discharged through a cloth hose attached to the lower rear end of the *pipa*. These quaint, rolling tanks supplied the water needs of many of the poorer inhabitants of Brownsville until 1930, when an ordinance compelled all residents to utilize the city water system and banned *piperos* from the streets. Courtesy of the Brownsville Historical Association.

The boardwalk leading to the ferry to Matamoros. The entrance to the boardwalk was in downtown Brownsville on Levee Street, near Twelfth Street. Several small businesses lined both of its sides. The wooden planks led southward to a spot where the U.S. Customs House was located and where a barge was lashed to the riverbank. From the barge passengers were loaded aboard skiffs and rowed to the Mexican side of the Rio Grande.

Despite the existence beginning in 1910 of a nearby international railroad bridge that also served pedestrian and vehicular traffic, the ferry remained in operation until 1928, when the new Gateway Bridge was opened to connect downtown Brownsville with Matamoros. Courtesy of the Brownsville Historical Association.

The Stillman house, Brownsville. Runyon developed a keen interest in U.S. and Mexican history and over the years acquired a historical library that exceeded one hundred volumes. His love for history can often be detected from his photographs. The home of Charles Stillman, the founder of Brownsville, was built in 1850 of local hand-made brick with a New England slate shingle roof. Stillman, a native of Connecticut who migrated to the Lower Rio Grande Valley before the Mexican-American War, recognized that the acquisition of the northern side of the Rio Grande by the United States greatly increased the potential of the region for development. Accordingly, in 1850 he purchased a large tract of land adjoining Fort Brown and formed a company to establish a town that he named in honor of Major Jacob Brown, who died in an artillery exchange between Mexican and U.S. forces on May 9, 1846. The Stillman house has been painstakingly restored and currently serves as a regional historical museum supported by the Brownsville Historical Association. Courtesy of the Barker Texas History Center.

STRET SCENE, MERCEDES TEXAS.

Mercedes street scene, c. 1915. Few of today's residents of Mercedes, thirty-five miles northwest of Brownsville, would recognize this picture. Fortunately, however, Runyon's photographic excursions through the Lower Valley to supply the postcard needs of local merchants provide us with an invaluable record of what the cities and towns of the region looked like in the second and third decades of the twentieth century. Courtesy of the Barker Texas History Center.

San Benito street scene, c. 1914. Because of the existence of photographs like this one, scholars interested in the urban architecture, the modes of transportation, the styles of dress, and even the condition of the city streets during this era have a primary source to interpret. Courtesy of the Barker Texas History Center.

Drugstore soda fountain, c. 1912. The proprietor and his employees proudly pose for Runyon's camera. Note the postcard rack on the counter to the left. During the postcard era in the United States retail merchants sold them virtually everywhere: bookstores, curio shops, drugstores, variety stores, stationery stores, department stores, cigar stores, hotel lobbies, and street corner newsstands. Courtesy of the Barker Texas History Center.

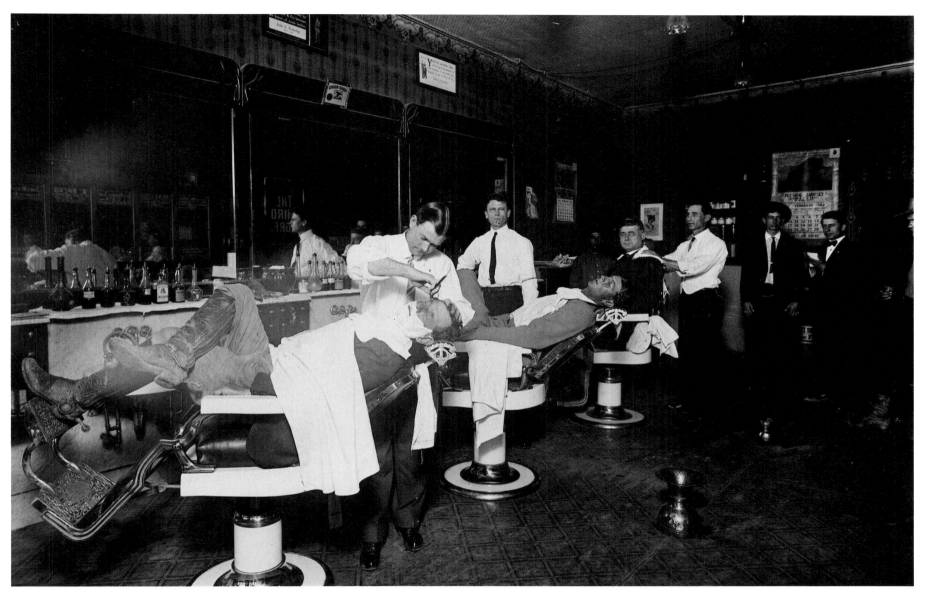

Barbershop scene, Brownsville. This picture recalls a time when middle-class businessmen not only went to the barbershop every few weeks for a haircut but daily, except weekends and holidays, for a shave and some conversation. Courtesy of the Barker Texas History Center.

Although Creager announced before Harding's arrival that his visit was strictly private, local leaders refused to allow the soon-to-be twenty-ninth president of the United States to get away without some festivities. They organized a big parade through the streets of downtown Brownsville that ended on the parade ground of Fort Brown. There Harding delivered some informal remarks to 60,000 people who came to see him from all over the Valley and northeastern Mexico. This car, decorated with flowers, was part of the parade. Courtesy of the Barker Texas History Center.

Newspaper readers in many parts of the United States saw this Runyon picture of Warren G. Harding (left) and R. B. Creager standing on the front porch of the latter's Brownsville home. The president-elect arrived on November 6, 1920, for a postelection rest at the invitation of Creager, a close personal friend and the Republican National Committeeman from Texas. During his visit to the Lower Rio Grande Valley, Harding stayed at Creager's homes in Brownsville and Point Isabel (now Port Isabel), where he went to do some fishing. Courtesy of the Barker Texas History Center.

Brownsville High School girls' basketball team, 1926. As the official photographer for the Brownsville High School yearbook, the *Palmetto*, from 1918 to 1926, Runyon took hundreds of pictures like this one of athletic teams and extracurricular organizations. Courtesy of the Barker Texas History Center.

The land development companies paid owners of showplaces to receive home seekers and tell them of their success. Courtesy of the Barker Texas History Center.

LONE STAR IMMIGRATION COMPANY'S EXCURSION AT EL JARDIN CABBAGE PATCH FEB 11th 1920

The decade after the First World War was a period of rapid population growth in the Lower Rio Grande Valley, thanks in part to the efforts of real estate development company promoters, who lured prospects from northern states and even Canada to the area on excursions. The Lone Star Immigration Company and other organizations like it had extremely efficient sales operations. Recruiting agents traveled widely to tout the wonders of life in what they called "the Magic Valley of Texas" to potential settlers or "home seekers." Many of the agents were highly experienced and had done similar work in the Cherokee strip of Oklahoma in 1899. They invited interested individuals to view the "paradisiacal region" for

themselves on organized tours. Since most prospective customers were farmers from the north, the prime excursion season was during the winter, when the farmers had more free time and when the warm Valley weather and the crops growing in the fields were likely to make a favorable impression. The home seekers arrived in chartered railroad cars in groups as large as three hundred. Men were encouraged to bring their wives along in order to eliminate the need to postpone purchase agreements until they could return home to discuss the matter. Although land company agents tried to collect whatever they could from home seekers, the development companies usually wound up heavily subsidizing most excursions, which in-

cluded not only the cost of transportation but of food and lodging in the Lower Valley. From the moment the excursionists arrived, agents of the company sponsoring their trip jealously guarded them from rival landmen and from dissatisfied settlers. They herded the home seekers into automobiles for visits to carefully selected showplaces like this El Jardin cabbage patch, where the prospects could see for themselves the success one man had achieved after only a few short years of effort. Much to the delight of Runyon, who took this picture with his Kodak Circuit camera, the land development companies customarily provided the home seekers with complimentary souvenir group photographs prior to their departure for home. Courtesy of the Barker Texas History Center.

First communion. During the decade in which Runyon did portrait work, thousands of residents of the area visited his studio to have their pictures taken. Collectively these photographs provide social historians with valuable information about the lives of ordinary people during the period. Courtesy of the Barker Texas History Center.

Wedding portrait. When customers came to his studio to have their portraits made, Runyon had on display for their inspection a variety of frames that he made with his own special equipment. For an additional charge he gladly framed his clients' portraits. Courtesy of the Barker Texas History Center.

People of all ages, ethnic backgrounds, and occupations, including this railroad worker holding his lantern, came to Runyon's studio to have their portraits made. Courtesy of the Barker Texas History Center.

In an era when organized labor enjoyed but scant success in Texas, the presence of a sizable number of federal civilian workers at Fort Brown and with the U.S. Immigration Service enabled the National Federation of Federal Employees to establish a foothold in Brownsville. Courtesy of the Barker Texas History Center.

Lillian (b. March 1914), Amali (b. November 1915), and Virginia Runyon (b. September 1917) in a field of flowers near their home in Brownsville on March 12, 1919. When Robert Runyon wanted to test a new camera, lens, or the latest processing chemicals, he frequently went into the backyard of his home and took a picture using his children as subjects despite their dirty faces and old playclothes. On this occasion, however, his girls were dressed in their Sunday best. This beautiful picture seems to convey the photographer's love for his three young daughters. Courtesy of the Barker Texas History Center.

ECHINOCEREUS PENTALOPHUS.   Copyright, R. Runyon. 530

Runyon was also fond of several species of the *Echinocereus* including the *Echinocereus pentalophus*, which he photographed in full flower (c. 1920) in order to make this lovely postcard. The production of this card demonstrates very clearly the link between Runyon's profession as a photographer and his interest in the flora of the Lower Rio Grande Valley as a hobby. Courtesy of the Library of the University of Texas of the Permian Basin, Special Collections.

The *Nymphaea elegans* was one of Runyon's favorite wildflowers. In his *Vernacular Names of Plants Indigenous to the Lower Rio Grande Valley of Texas,* he wrote affectionately of this water lily that he had observed and photographed so often in the field: ". . . with their delicate pale blue flowers [they] attract the attention of all those who love wild flowers" (p. vii). Courtesy of the Barker Texas History Center.

1. Robert Runyon: Border Photographer

1. Robert Runyon, *Supplement to Runyon Genealogy,* p. xx; Robert Runyon, *Mirror Plater's Guide;* Amali R. Perkins, interview, San Antonio, Sept. 24, 1988; William T. Runyon to Lillian R. Mahoney, Fort Worth, June 20, 1963, Robert Runyon Document File, Barker Texas History Center, University of Texas at Austin (hereafter cited as BTHC); [Robert Runyon], "History, Data, and Information Relative to Robert Runyon, P. O. Box 11, Brownsville, Texas," pp. 1, 4, BTHC.

2. Runyon, *Supplement to Runyon Genealogy,* p. xx; Delbert Runyon, interview, Brownsville, July 28, 1989; Amali R. Perkins, interview, San Antonio, Sept. 24, 1989.

3. Jacob L. Stambaugh and Lillian Stambaugh, *The Lower Rio Grande Valley of Texas,* p. 318; Richard T. Marcum, "Fort Brown, Texas: The History of a Border Post," p. 273.

4. Ruby A. Wooldridge and Robert A. Vezzetti, *Brownsville: A Picture History,* p. 84.

5. Stambaugh and Stambaugh, *The Lower Rio Grande Valley,* pp. 231, 318–319. Because of the population growth of the Rio Grande Valley, the Texas Legislature redivided the area to create an additional county, Willacy County, before the 1930 census.

6. See Henry Lindemann to Robert Runyon, Denver, Colo., Dec. 28, 1909, BTHC; Francis L. Lester Company to Robert Runyon, Mesilla, N. Mex., Aug. 31, 1910, BTHC; W. H. Tammen Company to Robert Runyon, Denver, Colo., Sept. 29, 1910, BTHC; Henry J. Beach to Robert Runyon, El Paso, Jan. 4, 1910, BTHC.

7. Amali R. Perkins, interview, San Antonio, Sept. 24, 1988; Kodak Exposure Records of Robert Runyon, Dec. 12, 1907–Feb. 9, 1909, BTHC.

8. See North American Post Card Company to Robert Runyon, Kansas City, Mo., May 3, 1910, BTHC; Detroit Publishing Company to Robert Runyon, Detroit, Mich., Oct. 29, 1910, BTHC; Elite Post Card Company to Robert Runyon, Kansas City, Mo., Nov. 8, 1910, BTHC.

9. C. V. Williams Photograph Company to Robert Runyon, Bloomington, Ind., Sept. 30, 1910, BTHC. Also see C. V. Williams Company to Robert Runyon, Bloomington, Ind., Oct. 31, 1910, BTHC.

10. William T. Runyon to Lillian R. Mahoney, Fort Worth, June 20, 1963, BTHC; Tom Jones to Robert Runyon, Cincinnati, Ohio, Sept. 7, 1910, Sept. 24, 1910, BTHC.

11. Robert Runyon to W. J. Lampton, Brownsville, Nov. 23, 1910, quoted in *Catlettsburg Tribune,* Nov. 30, 1910.

12. See Dorothy B. Ryan, *Picture Postcards in the United States, 1893–1918,* pp. 1–3, 15–16, 27–33, 61–68, 70, 87, 89, 91, 100–103, 105–111, 117–123, 127, 145, 151, 165–185; Frank Staff, *The Picture Postcard and Its Origins,* pp. 7, 49, 61–62, 67–80, 86; Paul J. Vanderwood and Frank N. Samponaro, *Border Fury: A Picture Postcard Record of Mexico's Revolution and U.S. War Preparedness, 1910–1917,* pp. 1–14; Hal Morgan and Andreas Brown, *Prairie Fires and Paper Moons: The American Photographic Postcard, 1900–1920,* pp. viii–xiv, 187; Richard Conniff, "When 'Friends' Pressed the Button, There Was No Place to Hide," *Smithsonian* 19 (June 1988): 106–117.

13. See Vanderwood and Samponaro, *Border Fury,* pp. 63–107.

14. Owl News and Cigar Store to Robert Runyon, Kingsville, Jan. 15, 1911, BTHC; Mercedes Drug Company to Robert Runyon, Mercedes, July 23, 1911, BTHC; Spottle and Steele, Jewelers and Opticians, to Robert Runyon, San Benito, Aug. 19, 1911, BTHC; James M. Rogers to Robert Runyon, McAllen, Jan. 17, 1912, BTHC.

15. Will H. Wood to Robert Runyon, Mission, Nov. 7, 1911, BTHC.

16. George E. Knauff, Gulf Coast News and Hotel Company, to Robert Runyon, San Antonio, June 17, 1911, Nov. 21, 1911, BTHC; R. O. Powell, Gulf Coast News and Hotel Company, to Robert Runyon, Houston, Oct. 14, 1911, Jan. 2, 1912, BTHC.

17. See "List of Postcards, All Property of Robert Runyon, Brownsville," n.d., BTHC; William T. Runyon to Lillian R. Mahoney, Fort Worth, June 20, 1963, BTHC.

18. C. V. Williams Company to Robert Runyon, Bloomington, Ind., Sept. 31, 1910, BTHC; Tom Jones to Robert Runyon, Cincinnati, Ohio, Dec. 17, 1910, Dec. 20, 1910, Dec. 28, 1910, Feb. 3, 1911, Feb. 11, 1911, April 1, 1911, Aug. 18, 1911, BTHC; Curt Teich and Company to Robert Runyon, Chicago, Sept. 12, 1911, Oct. 14, 1911, BTHC.

19. McBride Photo Supply Company to Robert Runyon, Houston, June 10, 1911, June 28, 1911, July 27, 1911, Aug. 12, 1911, BTHC.

20. Tom Jones to Robert Runyon, Cincinnati, Ohio, Aug. 1, 1911, BTHC.

21. Curt Teich and Company to Robert Runyon, Chicago, Sept. 12, 1911, BTHC. Also see Curt Teich and Company to Robert Runyon, Chicago, July 21, 1911, BTHC.

22. Ibid., Sept. 20, 1911, Dec. 2, 1911.

23. See W. B. Bottum to Robert Runyon, Mission, May 28, 1911, BTHC; Hatie Benthal to Robert Runyon, Pharr, Dec. 16, 1911, BTHC.

24. See Spittle and Steele, Jewelers and Opticians, to Robert Runyon, San Benito, Aug. 6, 1911, Aug. 10, 1911, BTHC; R .A. Jeffreys to Robert Runyon, Mission, Nov. 7, 1911, BTHC.

25. See Melado Land Company to Robert Runyon, Houston, July 30, 1911, Nov. 7, 1911, Nov. 28, 1911, Dec. 28, 1911, BTHC; Mrs. Houston Jones to Robert Runyon, Pharr, Dec. 19, 1911, BTHC; Delbert Runyon, interview, Brownsville, July 28, 1989.

26. Amali R. Perkins, interview, San Antonio, Sept. 24, 1988.

27. Gloeckner and Newby Company to Robert Runyon, New York, Sept. 11, 1911, Sept. 23, 1911, BTHC. No wide-angle lens could be satisfactorily used with Runyon's 3A Graflex. See Folmer and Schwing Division, Eastman Kodak Company, to Robert Runyon, Rochester, N.Y., June 30, 1911, BTHC.

28. Receipt for *Popular Photography* magazine to Robert Runyon, *Popular Photography*, Boston, Mass., Nov. 7, 1911, BTHC.

29. American Photographic Text Book Company to Robert Runyon, Scranton, Penn., June 8, 1911, Dec. 13, 1911, BTHC; Office of Superintendent of Documents, to Robert Runyon, Washington, D.C., Dec. 13, 1911, BTHC.

30. Poll tax receipt of Robert Runyon, State of Texas, County of Cameron, Jan. 22, 1912, in the possession of Delbert Runyon, Brownsville; [Runyon], "History, Data, and Information Relative to Robert Runyon," p. 1.

31. Amali R. Perkins, interview, San Antonio, Sept. 24, 1988.

32. *Brownsville Herald*, May 12, 1916; Marcum, "Fort Brown," p. 273.

33. *Brownsville Herald*, Feb. 17, 1913, Feb. 18, 1913; Frank C. Pierce, *A Brief History of the Lower Rio Grande Valley*, pp. 77–78; Stambaugh and Stambaugh, *The Lower Rio Grande Valley*, p. 208.

34. *Brownsville Herald*, Feb. 25, 1913, Feb. 26, 1913; Pierce, *A Brief History of the Lower Rio Grande Valley*, pp. 78–79; Marcum, "Fort Brown," p. 285. The Texas National Guardsmen remained in Brownsville until July 28, 1913; the Texas Rangers stayed indefinitely.

35. *Brownsville Herald*, Apr. 14, 1913.

36. Ibid., May 15, 1913, May 22, 1913.

37. Ibid., May 23, 1913, June 3, 1913, June 4, 1913.

38. See ibid., June 4, 1913, June 5, 1913; Pierce, *A Brief History of the Lower Rio Grande Valley*, pp. 80–82; Stambaugh and Stambaugh, *The Lower Rio Grande Valley*, p. 209.

39. *Brownsville Herald*, June 4, 1913.

40. *Valley Morning Star*, Mar. 7, 1952; see *Brownsville Herald*, June 5, 1913, June 9, 1913.

41. See *Valley Morning Star*, Mar. 7, 1952.

42. *Brownsville Herald*, Feb. 27, 1983; [Runyon], "History, Data, and Information Relative to Robert Runyon," pp. 4–5.

43. Delbert Runyon, interview, Brownsville, July 28, 1989; Amali R. Perkins, interview, San Antonio, Sept. 24, 1988; José C. Medrano to Robert Runyon, Matamoros, Mexico, Oct. 10, 1912, BTHC. Francisco

González Villarreal remained loyal to Carranza when Blanco split with him in late 1914 and thereafter rose rapidly in the ranks of the Mexican army. González was a brigade general and the commander of the garrison at Ciudad Juárez in mid-June 1919, when Pancho Villa made one final and unsuccessful attempt to take the border city. He was promoted to division general in the late 1930s by President Lázaro Cárdenas shortly before his retirement from the Mexican army. See Clarence C. Clendenen, *The United States and Pancho Villa: A Study in Unconventional Diplomacy*, p. 312; Delbert Runyon, interview, Brownsville, July 28, 1989.

44. See Curt Teich and Company to Robert Runyon, Chicago, Aug. 12, 1913, BTHC; Amali R. Perkins, interview, San Antonio, Sept. 24, 1988; Delbert Runyon, interview, Brownsville, July 28, 1989.

45. See *Brownsville Herald*, Sept. 1, 1913.

46. *Houston Post*, Sept. 4, 1913, Sept. 5, 1913, Sept. 8, 1913, Sept. 12, 1913, Sept. 21, 1913; *San Antonio Express*, Sept. 5, 1913, Sept. 6, 1913; L. Gutierrez de Lara and Edcumb Pinchon, *The Mexican People: Their Struggle for Freedom*, p. 42.

47. *Valley Morning Star*, Mar. 7, 1952; Delbert Runyon, interviews, Brownsville, Oct. 22, 1988, July 28, 1989.

48. *Valley Morning Star*, Mar. 7, 1952; invoice, Hill Sign Company to Robert Runyon, Brownsville, Dec. 2, 1913, BTHC; *Brownsville Herald*, Dec. 1, 1913, Dec. 2, 1913, Feb. 27, 1983. Glass lantern slides were positive photographic images on film used for projecting still pictures to a screen, especially in early motion picture theaters. They were frequently used for advertisements and news photographs. To protect the emulsion two thin pieces of glass were used as a cover and were secured by a cloth tape glued to the edges.

49. *Valley Morning Star*, Mar. 7, 1952; *Brownsville Herald*, Feb. 27, 1983.

50. Amali R. Perkins, interview, San Antonio, Sept. 24, 1988; [Runyon], "History, Data, and Information Relative to Robert Runyon," p. 4. In addition to William, born in 1904, and Lillian, born in 1914, Runyon had two other children to support by the fall of 1917. They were Amali, born on November 9, 1915, and Virginia, born on September 29, 1917.

51. *Brownsville Herald*, Apr. 6, 1916, May 12, 1916; Don M. Coerver and Linda B. Hall, *Texas and the Mexican Revolution: A Study in State and National Border Policy 1910–1920*, pp. 59, 64, 78, 87.

52. Delbert Runyon, interview, Brownsville, Oct. 22, 1988; Amali R. Perkins, interview, San Antonio, Sept.

24, 1988. Throughout his career as a professional photographer, Runyon preferred glass plate negatives to sheet or rolled film, which he regarded as a medium for amateurs. He thought that glass plate negatives were easier to wash and retouch and gave better results. See Delbert Runyon, interview, Brownsville, July 28, 1989.

53. Delbert Runyon, interview, Brownsville, Oct. 22, 1988; Amali R. Perkins, interview, San Antonio, Sept. 24, 1988; *Brownsville Herald*, June 28, 1916, July 1, 1916, July 6, 1916, July 13, 1916, July 18, 1916, July 27, 1916, Aug. 2, 1916, Aug. 18, 1916, Aug. 24, 1916, Sept. 4, 1916, Sept. 8, 1916.

54. "Robert Runyon: Commercial Photographer, Post Card and Souvenir Dealer, Brownsville" letterhead stationery, n.d., BTHC; Delbert Runyon, interview, Brownsville, Oct. 22, 1988; Amali R. Perkins, interview, San Antonio, Sept. 24, 1988.

55. Amali R. Perkins, interview, San Antonio, Sept. 24, 1988.

56. "Robert Runyon, Commercial Photographer, Post Card and Souvenir Dealer, Brownsville," letterhead stationery, n.d., BTHC.

57. Jim Dan Hill, *The Minute Man in Peace and War: A History of the National Guard*, p. 242; Vanderwood and Samponaro, *Border Fury*, p. 14.

58. See Brian Robertson, *Rio Grande Heritage: A Pictorial History*, p. 167; Wooldridge and Vezzetti, *Brownsville*, p. 100.

59. William T. Runyon to Lillian R. Mahoney, Fort Worth, June 20, 1963, BTHC.

60. Delbert Runyon, interview, Brownsville, July 28, 1989; Amali R. Perkins, interview, San Antonio, Sept. 24, 1988.

61. Ibid.

62. Inventory, Property of Robert Runyon, Photographer, Brownsville, Jan. 1, 1918, in the possession of Delbert Runyon, Brownsville.

63. Delbert Runyon, interview, Brownsville, July 28, 1989.

64. See Brownsville High School, *Palmetto*, for the period 1918–1926.

65. C. J. Ramsey to Robert Runyon, Point Isabel, June 29, 1918, BTHC; Dorothy Gill to Robert Runyon, McAllen, July 2, 1918, BTHC; Mabel Nelson to Robert Runyon, Kingsville, Nov. 1, 1918, BTHC; Eva H. Nash to Robert Runyon, Mission, Dec. 4, 1918, BTHC; Mabel Fink to Robert Runyon, McAllen, Jan. 14, 1919, BTHC; T. R. Henderson to Robert Runyon, Harlingen, Oct. 27, 1919, BTHC; Frank W. Roberts to Robert Runyon, San Benito, Oct. 9, 1918, BTHC; R. B. Hadden to Robert

Runyon, Mercedes, Nov. 13, 1918, BTHC; Robert Runyon to Commanding Officer, Fort Ringgold, Brownsville, Dec. 13, 1918, BTHC; Donna Drug Store to Robert Runyon, Donna, Oct. 18, 1919, BTHC; Curt Teich Company to Robert Runyon, Chicago, Mar. 13, 1925, Aug. 16, 1926, BTHC; Brownsville High School, *Palmetto*, 1924, p. 149; *Buried Treasure*, n.d., BTHC; *Rio Grande Valley, Herald of Progress: A Picture Journey through the Rio Grande Valley of Texas*, BTHC.

66. See the following Western Union telegrams: *Chicago Daily News* to Robert Runyon, Chicago, Nov. 6, 1920; Underwood and Underwood, Inc., to Robert Runyon, New York, Nov. 6, 1920; Central News Photo Service to Robert Runyon, New York, Nov. 8, 1920; *Dallas Morning News* to Robert Runyon, Dallas, Nov. 30, 1920; *New York Times* to Robert Runyon, New York, Nov. 5, 1920, BTHC.

67. Underwood and Underwood to Robert Runyon, New York, Nov. 15, 1920, BTHC; *New York Times* to Robert Runyon, New York, Dec. 4, 1920, BTHC; *Houston Chronicle* to Robert Runyon, Houston, Dec. 3, 1920, BTHC; *Dallas Morning News* to Robert Runyon, Dallas, Nov. 30, 1920, BTHC.

68. *Houston Chronicle*, Mar. 7, 1921–Mar. 12, 1921, Jan. 1, 1922, Jan. 22, 1923; *Houston Post*, Dec. 19, 1926; *Monty's Monthly: A Periodical of and for the Valley*, Sept. 1919, Nov.–Dec. 1920, Aug. 1927; *Texas Commercial News*, Nov. 29, 1924.

69. Robert Runyon to Inspector in Charge, Immigration Service, Brownsville, May 1923, BTHC.

70. Lillian R. Mahoney, interview, Austin, Oct. 20, 1989.

71. For example, see Jonathan Fallowfield to Robert Runyon, London, England, May 13, 1921, Mar. 14, 1923, May 13, 1923, BTHC; also see Appendix A.

72. See G. H. Pittman and Brothers to Robert Runyon, Dallas, Sept. 1, 1926, BTHC; O. K. Pharmacy to Robert Runyon, Edinburg, Nov. 9, 1926, BTHC; Delbert Runyon, interview, Brownsville, Oct. 22, 1988; Amali R. Perkins, interview, San Antonio, Sept. 24, 1988.

73. Delbert Runyon, interview, Brownsville, July 28, 1989; Amali R. Perkins, interview, San Antonio, Sept. 24, 1988.

74. Delbert Runyon, interview, Brownsville, July 28, 1989.

75. Ibid.; Robert A. Runyon, interview, Brownsville, July 28, 1989; Amali R. Perkins, interview, San Antonio, Sept. 24, 1988; Lillian R. Mahoney, interview, Austin, Oct. 20, 1989; *Brownsville Herald*, Mar. 10, 1968; business address book of Robert Runyon, Brownsville, 1934, in the possession of Delbert Runyon, Brownsville; Southwest Medical Society, "Program of the Fifth and Sixth Districts," El Jardin Hotel, Brownsville, July 2–3, 1936, BTHC.

76. See Sanders' Variety and Art Store to Robert Runyon, Harlingen, Mar. 5, 1927, BTHC; Weslaco Drug Company to Robert Runyon, Weslaco, Apr. 23, 1927, BTHC; J. B. Malone to Robert Runyon, Mission, Aug. 28, 1928, BTHC; List of Accounts of Robert Runyon, Brownsville, Aug. 31, 1927, BTHC. Also see Seabold Invisible Camera Corporation to Robert Runyon, Rochester, N.Y., Mar. 15, 1928, BTHC.

77. G. H. Pittman and Brothers to Robert Runyon, Dallas, June 30, 1927, BTHC; Curt Teich and Company to Robert Runyon, Chicago, Jan. 24, 1936, Sept. 2, 1936, Sept. 28, 1936, BTHC.

78. Curt Teich and Company, "Geographic Index for Brownsville, Texas, 1911–1940," Curt Teich Postcard Collection, Lake County Museum, Wauconda, Ill.

79. Delbert Runyon, interview, Brownsville, July 28, 1989.

80. Tom Jones to Robert Runyon, Cincinnati, Ohio, June 7, 1910, BTHC.

81. Ibid., Sept. 7, 1910, Oct. 3, 1910.

82. U.S. Library of Congress, *Expl. Circular*, No. 35, July 1925, BTHC.

83. For example, see Register of Copyrights, Library of Congress to Robert Runyon, Washington, D.C., Oct. 10, 1910, BTHC; Robert Runyon to Register of Copyrights, Library of Congress, Brownsville, Dec. 23, 1910, Aug. 23, 1911, Aug. 1, 1923, BTHC; Curt Teich and Company to Robert Runyon, Chicago, Dec. 24, 1927, BTHC. Also see J. M. Stein to Robert Runyon, Brownsville, Jan. 2, 1925, BTHC.

84. Incontrovertible evidence exists among Runyon's negatives in the Barker Texas History Center to indicate that he pirated the image made by an unknown photographer of Emiliano Zapata and two of Walter Horne's postcards with scenes of combat during the second battle of Ciudad Juárez in 1913.

85. Robert Runyon to O. F. Williams, Brownsville, Aug. 22, 1938, BTHC; Amali R. Perkins, interview, San Antonio, Sept. 24, 1988.

86. H. L. Yates to Robert Runyon, Brownsville, June 6, 1927, Dec. 12, 1927, BTHC.

87. C. G. Malott to Robert Runyon, San Antonio, Mar. 30, 1928, BTHC; Robert E. Cofer to Robert Runyon, San Antonio, June 4, 1928, BTHC.

88. Robert E. Cofer to Robert Runyon, San Antonio, Nov. 13, 1928, BTHC. Runyon bought and read the pertinent parts of two books on copyright law: George Haven Putnam, *The Question of Copyright*; and Hugh K. Wagner, *Damages, Profits, and Accounting in Patent, Copyright, Trademark, and Unfair Competition Cases*.

89. U.S. National Archives, Southwestern Region, Record Group 21, Records of U.S. District Courts, Southern District of Texas, Brownsville, N. 552 at Law; Delbert Runyon, interview, Brownsville, July 28, 1989.

90. "Robert Runyon for Mayor," press release, n.d., BTHC.

91. *Brownsville Herald*, Mar. 10, 1968; [Runyon], "History, Data, and Information Relative to Robert Runyon," p. 1.

92. For information on the often stormy and controversial political career of Robert Runyon, see *Brownsville Herald*, Dec. 27, 1937, Jan. 16, 1942, Mar. 19, 1942, Aug. 2, 1942, Oct. 1, 1942, Nov. 2, 1942, Mar. 16, 1943, Sept. 3, 1950.

93. Minnie Gilbert, "R. Runyon and His 'Little Hunk of the World,'" in *Roots by the River: A Story of Texas Tropical Borderland Valley, By-Liners*, ed. Teresa Chapa Alamía and Elena Farías Barrera, 2: 223–227; Joe Ideker, "Robert Runyon, Pioneer Lower Rio Grande Valley Botanist," *Sabal* 5 (Dec. 1988): 1–5; *Brownsville Herald*, Feb. 27, 1983.

94. Gilbert, "R. Runyon," 2: 223–227; Amali R. Perkins, interview, San Antonio, Sept. 24, 1988; Ideker, "Robert Runyon," p. 3.

95. Gilbert, "R. Runyon," 2: 223–226; Ideker, "Robert Runyon," pp. 4–5; *San Antonio Evening News*, Apr. 11, 1947; *Brownsville Herald*, Feb. 27, 1983; Delbert Runyon, interview, Brownsville, July 28, 1989.

96. Delbert Runyon, interview, Brownsville, July 28, 1989.

97. *Brownsville Herald*, Mar. 10, 1968.

2. Runyon Records the Mexican Revolution

The Mexican Revolution sputtered to a start in late 1910. Francisco Madero, a propertied man as well as a spiritualist, saw his electoral bid for the nation's presidency frustrated by the brute force of the reigning dictatorship, and set the date of November 20 for a general uprising. Hardly anyone responded. Only in western Chihuahua, where foothills meld into the majestic Sierra Madre, did some rancheros fight the federal army to a standstill. Their activities gradually encouraged Mexicans elsewhere to join the struggle, and within three or four months battles raged in various locations. In May 1911 the revolutionaries triumphed and sent the dictator, Porfirio Díaz, packing.

Victory, however, did not bring peace. With Madero's fledgling government unable to fulfill the strident demands of its factionalized constituents, new revolts erupted. Rebels took to arms in the name of their regional and/or ideological leaders: *orozquistas* and *vasquistas* in the north, *magonistas* over in Baja California and *zapatistas* in the south.

Recent scholarship views these disparate rebellions as the start of a widespread popular uprising.[1] Nevertheless, large areas of Mexico remained relatively calm during these tumultuous times, such as around Matamoros and Brownsville, where Robert Runyon did his photography. Naturally, people in the region were excited by national events, but they did not openly wish to choose sides and to take to the field. Instead, they hung out the sign "Business as usual."

"Business" in the Lower Rio Grande had always included a good deal of smuggling, and the advent of revolution in Mexico provided an unparalleled opportunity to increase such trade. Guns, ammunition, horses, all sorts of war matériel were needed to sustain the fighting, and people from the region were only too willing to service the high demand.

The U.S. government, diplomatically friendly to Díaz's beleaguered dictatorship and then to Madero, tried to stop the smuggling with bombast and proclamations, but never could back up the words with the qualified manpower necessary to properly police the easily penetrated border. Precisely what sorts of activities constituted neutrality violations became logjammed in a sticky legal argument.[2] While lawyers debated the issue before judges, business opportunists continued to profit on both sides of the frontier. When the U.S. consul in Matamoros reported on March 21, 1911, that people in the area were "excited" and "are trying to make best of troubles now existing throughout the republic," he correctly, but perhaps unwittingly, characterized the profiteering that flourished.[3]

Despite their financial windfall, residents of Matamoros and Brownsville were justifiably concerned about their livelihood and personal safety. Rebels, regardless of their stamp, recognized the need to capture and control a border city in order to regularize their matériel requirements. Such an accomplishment might also lead the United States to grant them belligerency status, which would really open up the supply floodgates. Madero had concentrated on Ciudad Juárez and El Paso, and the capture of Juárez may have given the final nudge to the dictatorship. Rumors that Matamoros would soon be attacked by rebels kept residents there on edge and caused both

Mexican and U.S. authorities to reinforce, as best they could, their respective security forces.[4]

While Madero won the war, he could not impose peace. Reports of impending counterrevolutionary attacks on Matamoros were especially rife in late 1911, when an old friend of the dictatorship, Bernardo Reyes, a respected army general who in previous years had developed his power base in the north, began to plot against Madero from southern Texas. In fact, Reyes crossed into Mexico upriver from Matamoros in November 1911, but his armed support failed to materialize; he was captured and then jailed in Mexico City. But within a year Matamoros would hear more from Reyes and his coconspirators.

Throughout the early months of Madero's tenure, conditions in Matamoros continued to smolder. The U.S. consul there noted at one time that satisfaction with political events seemed to prevail but at another, that people expressed reservations about a government from which they had received no direct benefit. In late 1912 word spread that the *vasquistas* were marching on the city; if indeed they were, they never arrived.[5]

Meanwhile, at the center of turmoil in Mexico City, conditions worsened for the Madero government. On February 9, 1913, Bernardo Reyes, freed from prison by coconspirators and in the company of Félix Díaz, a nephew of the deposed dictator, rebelled against Madero in the capital itself, and so began what has become known in Mexican history as the Decena Trágica, the Ten Tragic Days. The contest remained stalemated for five days until the federal commander, Victoriano Huerta, chosen to defend the government, instead defected to the enemy with the connivance of the U.S. ambassador, Henry Lane Wilson. The murder of President Madero and his vice-president quickly followed; Huerta became the new president, and within a month groups of outraged citizens took up arms against him.

Not everywhere, of course. Some citizens endorsed the change. In Matamoros, for example, on February 17, in the midst of the challenge in Mexico City, federal troops led by Major Esteban Ramos, a longtime friend of Félix Díaz, rebelled in favor of his friends and arrested the elected city officials. Not a shot was fired, and the consul

reported that throughout the coup the citizenry had remained calm. Prisoners were soon released and business returned to normal. At the same time the consul dismissed annoying accounts that Major Ramos and his troops extorted money from wealthy locals, including Americans, by threatening to send his cavalry out to pasture and to turn the city over to less disciplined troops who would presumably loot it.[6] Texas governor Oscar B. Colquitt ordered additional state guardsmen to Brownsville just in case and told their officer in charge: "Notify the Mexican commander at Matamoros that if he harms a single Texan, his life will be demanded as forfeit."[7]

Governor Colquitt had engaged in such hyperbole ever since the revolution erupted along the border. Raids back and forth across the international line had put the lives and property of Texans in jeopardy, and he believed it his duty to protect them. Although he insisted that the federal government had the responsibility to assure the safety of all U.S. citizens and their holdings, Colquitt decried inadequacies of the administration in Washington, D.C., rambunctiously formulated his own border policy, and sent the Texas Rangers and the state guard to enforce it. Such a strident stance often put Colquitt at odds with the nation's top administrators and diplomats as well as the country's military field commanders. Washington's biggest fear was that Colquitt would actually order his state forces across the line into Mexico to avenge some perceived wrong, which in fact, he threatened to do.[8]

When federal troops arrived at Brownsville unannounced to any state officials, the governor told their commander, General E. Z. Steever: "I hope your instructions from Washington will not require you to interfere with the orderly discharge of their duty by state troops which have been forwarded to Brownsville." By that he meant that, if federal forces tried to stop the Texas troops from crossing into Mexico, they would have a fight on their hands. Colquitt emphasized: "We will not hesitate to use state troops to protect Texas people."[9]

Fortunately for all involved, Governor Colquitt never ordered his state forces into Mexico. In fact, at several points he reproved militiamen who strained at their leash. But he never stopped criticizing the national leaders for their border policies. Even as he stepped down from the governor's chair in January 1915, Colquitt labeled President Woodrow Wilson's administration "the greatest failure in the history of the presidency." He called Wilson's foreign policy "imbecilic" and his handling of Mexican affairs an "egregious failure."[10]

Indeed, Wilson was having his problems with the Mexicans—specifically, Victoriano Huerta, the usurper who refused to step down and heed the U.S. president's call for fair elections. Huerta's intransigence had Wilson looking around for a more manageable faction to support his political and socioeconomic intentions among his southern neighbor. Wilson's possible choices in mid-1914 centered upon Emiliano Zapata and his agrarian-minded adherents in the south, the unpredictable and unruly Pancho Villa around Chihuahua, and the Constitutionalists headed by a potentially difficult nationalist, Venustiano Carranza, who controlled much of the northeast. Not much choice for President Wilson among these three.[11]

As Wilson pondered, the Constitutionalist commander, Lucio Blanco, campaigned in Tamaulipas; by March he was on the Rio Grande and headed for Matamoros. Blanco hailed from Carranza's home state of Coahuila, where in 1879 he was the first of ten children born to Bernardo and María Blanco. His great grandfather had been governor of the state in the 1820s and a great-uncle had served as minister of war to President Benito Juárez in the 1860s. Blanco's father, Bernardo, a rancher and large landowner around the village of Múzquiz, sent Lucio to a private academy where the young student learned English and garnered a feel for national politics.[12]

While in his mid-twenties, Blanco helped Francisco Madero test the electoral laws in Coahuila and flirted with radical leftists known as *magonistas*, who were overtly dedicated to overthrowing the dictatorship. He fought in Madero's ranks and received an appointment to the Ministry of the Interior, but Blanco could not get along with his superiors and returned to Coahuila. There he earned his military spurs fighting against those who would unseat Madero and joined the Constitutionalists in response to Huerta's coup.[13]

Along his political and military path, Lucio Blanco developed a strong sentiment for poor, common people and appreciated their urgent need for agrarian reform. He advocated the elimination of debts among the worst off and security for both rural and urban workers. In articulating his program, Blanco condemned the wealthy, the bourgeoisie, and the clergy. Along with his equally radicalized sidekick, Francisco Múgica, he tried to persuade his Constitutionalist chief, Carranza, to liberalize his political programs to favor land reform and social justice. Carranza demurred, pleading for time.[14] Blanco sensed the need for more immediate action, so when assigned to spearhead the Constitutionalist rebellion in the northeastern state of Tamaulipas, he followed his own inclinations; he freed debt peons and initiated other land and labor reforms. In May 1913 he followed the Rio Grande, driving on Matamoros (population 10,000), a strategically critical border city needed by the Constitutionalists to better supply their revolution.

Blanco was a no-nonsense military commander. When federal soldiers taken prisoner in the capture of Reynosa (some forty miles west of Matamoros) declined to join his army, he ordered a dozen of them executed. Among them was an American, Juan Alamia, who had apparently sided with the federals. Alamia claimed he had just crossed the river to round up some horses he had pastured there, but Blanco thought him a spy and had him hanged.[15] About the same time, another American, Captain Everette Anglin, who had worked in law enforcement around McAllen, Texas, crossed the Rio Grande to claim some horses he had bought from a Mexican rancher. When Blanco refused him the horses, saying that he needed the mounts for his own troops, Anglin reminded him that the animals were U.S. property. In response, Blanco showed Captain Anglin the body of Alamia, dangling from a mesquite tree. Anglin got the message and returned to Texas without his horses.[16]

Constitutionalists frequented Brownsville's cantinas; they held strategy sessions downtown in the Dittman Theater. On May 31 Blanco arrived with some 1,500 largely ill-trained troops at Las Rucias, a rancho just west of Matamoros. From there he issued a forty-eight-hour surrender ultimatum to the federal commander, Major Esteban Ramos, called out of retirement to defend the city.

Blanco guaranteed the safety of all who surrendered their weapons but no such assurances for those who did not. He urged foreigners to leave the city and vowed not to damage the U.S. Consulate until Mexican defenders occupied it. Then he would bomb them out. Many citizens of Matamoros did not await the reply; they fled in terror to the safety of neighboring Brownsville on the U.S. side of the border. (In fact, the exodus brought some of the best families of Tamaulipas to the Valley, where they took up residence for good.) Major Ramos proved more steadfast; with 500 soldiers, plus a number of civilian volunteers, he dug in for the defense.[17]

Actually, the mayor of Matamoros, a medical doctor named Miguel F. Barragán, directed the frantic building of fortifications. Old breastworks constructed during the years of the French Intervention of the 1860s were reinforced, and four old cannons used as hitching posts on the corners of the main plaza were dug up and readied for action. The mayor's workers also erected barricades along the principal streets of the city with special attention paid to the electrical power and waterworks plants. Dr. Barragán also meant to interdict any intruders by means of electrical wires planted around town and reinforced by dynamite pits which could be activated at an appropriate moment. He also enlisted a good many sharpshooters into the ranks, men accustomed to deer hunting in the region. As his coup de grace Dr. Barragán dug up a cannon—probably of Mexican War vintage—which had been a landmark in front of the Cannon Grocery Store, had it cleaned and mounted in a cradle of mesquite logs, and pronounced the antique ready for action. No one knows where he got ammunition for this relic, but the regular army imported 10,000 rifle rounds from Brownsville. The battle lines were drawn; Major Ramos did not bother to respond to Blanco's ultimatum, and on June 3, 1913, the issue was joined.[18]

An eyewitness recounted the bitter battle which followed. Much of Brownsville turned out for the fight about to erupt across the river. They understood the danger of bullets zinging about, but the people of Brownsville, perched on top of hotels and stores and packed around the U.S. Customs House and International Bridge, strained to get a better view of the conflict. William A. Neale stood among the curious onlookers on top of the customs house, and he later wrote in his memoirs:

Precisely at ten o'clock a.m. the bugles of the invading army blew "The Advance." It was a beautiful sight to see how the invaders advanced towards the breastworks where their foes were waiting for them. No sooner did they reach the Cow Pens when volley after volley "spit out" flames of destruction. You could see the invaders' lines waver as they were being mowed down from the deadly fire of deer hunters whose aim and fire steadily thinned their ranks. . . . Three charges were made and three times they were repulsed. At last, however, part of Blanco's army got into the city.[19]

Neale witnessed acts of heroism: Blanco had ordered Colonel Cesáreo Castro to destroy the water tank that not only furnished water to the defenders, but provided water to the boilers of the engine which produced electricity for the wires to the dynamite pits. Colonel Castro at the head of some one hundred men riddled the water tank with bullets and soon put it out of commission. Then, in Neale's words, "Col. Castro with what few men he had left, at a double quick time, charged a small fort that was built on the left side of the International Bridge . . . . While advancing, his men were shot down one by one until he could not have had more than twenty-five men left as he reached the bridge. Then the defenders of the fort flew over to the American side of the river for protection. Upon reaching and taking possession of the [railroad] bridge, Colonel Castro dropped to his knees, then fell face down." Neale says he then saw to it that his "friend" Colonel Castro received a drink of water, so we know who William Neale, at least in retrospect, favored in this fight.[20]

By four o'clock in the afternoon Blanco's attack had forced the defenders back to their main position around the central plaza in town. Neale saw Dr. Barragán's pride go up in smoke: "The cannon that was propped on logs fired the first shot all OK., but when it fired the second time, you could see nothing but pieces of iron and lumber flying through the air. It appears that the second bag of five pounds of powder was dynamite that was inserted into the cannon as a load. When ignited it blew up and killed three of the men who were handling the cannon."[21] Soon after Major Ramos, seriously wounded when a bullet passed through his right side, retreated to Brownsville with some ninety of his men. The flight of Ramos left Marcial Garza Rivas in command. With the outcome no longer in doubt, just before dawn the *mariscal* told his troops to save themselves as they might. Some escaped to Brownsville, others through the enemy lines to the south. About sixty others were taken prisoner.[22]

J. L. Allhands, another witness to the battle from the Brownsville side, spotted Dr. Barragán, "harried and hunted," among the woebegone refugees. "After a thrilling escape, death ran with him to the river bank, but did not claim him, and with an expert on either side he swam that stream and took up his abode in the city of Brownsville." And so ended the bloody battle of Matamoros. "There was no Red Cross to care for the bruised and wounded in the stricken area. After this battle two huge funeral pyres were heaped high with 170 corpses, in Matamoros' streets of misery and debris, and partially burned. Even Brownsville, whose sanitary conditions were none too good, was menaced by the threat of pestilence from those partially burned, festering bodies."[23]

Brownsville absorbed the refugees as best it could. Residents such as Dr. W. F. Cole pleaded for toleration: ". . . a brave and civilized people we . . . . extend to the Mexican citizens who are sojourning among us our sympathy and generous and courteous treatment." The doctor noted that the majority of the local population had blood ties to Mexicans, and "for this reason if for no other we should avoid offense." He urged "patience and charity to those people who have been driven to seek refuge among us by the exigencies of war." Dr. Cole assured that many of his friends were Mexicans or of Mexican descent, and declared them "characterized by the virtues, charity, patience and generosity."[24]

While nervous citizens of Brownsville promoted a level-headed hospitality for the refugees, Blanco reveled in his victory across the river; Carranza even promoted him to general. His officers, Major

Emiliano P. Nafarrate, of whom we shall learn a great deal more in the following chapter, and Captain Otilio Falcón had enemy prisoners publicly executed, some twenty-five of them, including teenaged boys, who had volunteered to defend the city. On June 7 his men captured twenty-three-year-old Colonel Antonio Echazaretta, who commanded the volunteers, fourteen miles south of the city and returned him for execution at half past eight the next morning. Robert Runyon recorded the spectacle: Echazaretta in his last words regretted that he could die only once [for his country?], and even his captors lauded his coolness and bravery. They called him a "valiente muchacho." The executions revulsed even his admirers, so Blanco later blamed the senseless revenge on subordinates.[25]

Meanwhile, Blanco fortified the main plaza of Matamoros, which Huerta promised to retake but never attacked. He also made friends with Americans across the line, especially the director at the customs house, Frank Rabb, who made sure that a steady supply of war matériel flowed to the *carrancistas*. U.S. general James Parker, who had watched the attack from Brownsville, congratulated Blanco for his military tactics, and citizens who had fled the city gradually returned along with a good many American sightseers, despite the change in political leadership. The *maderista* mayor, Casimiro Sada, returned to office, and it was soon business as usual in Matamoros.[26]

The Constitutionalists went out of their way to protect U.S. interests. For example, Blanco returned to an American rancher with pasturage in Mexico the ninety-nine horses that his troops had confiscated from him en route to the city, and to insure a direct communications link to the United States, he asked the Southwestern Telegraph & Telephone Company to install a line from his headquarters to outlets across the border. The general also curried the favor of a few leading American businessmen at a Sunday luncheon he sponsored at a leading Brownsville restaurant. His guests reported "a very delightful and thoroughly cordial time."[27]

Jesse Johnson, the U.S. consul at Matamoros, reported:

. . . the Constitutionalists were under perfect discipline after the battle and have been ever since. This was true to such a great extent that when the battle was over . . . the Constitutionalists did not even break into drug stores to procure bandages and medicine for their wounded comrades.

General Blanco has wonderful control over his soldiers. Since the capture of Matamoros the city has been quieter and in better order than it has been before in many years. The property of foreigners has been respected and protected ever since the Constitutionalists forces have been in possession of Matamoros.[28]

The American press found Blanco personally attractive: "As soon as you look at General Blanco you are attracted to him. A keen dark eye, broad forehead, high cheek bones, a firm chin, a mouth denoting affection and compassion. A nose denoting acquisitiveness and great executive ability. A roach of black hair tinged with grey. Forty-seven, if a day, rotund, muscular, well set up, a bearing denoting ease, assurance, complacency, energy, command, courage, capacity, expediency, a well chosen leader of men."[29]

Some women, however, may have had their reservations about him, especially his air of mystery and seductiveness. The Runyon children remember their mother telling them about the sumptuous dance which Blanco gave in Matamoros. One of her girlfriends danced with the general but later that evening became quite ill. Later, when the young lady had recovered, companions explained to her (somewhat in jest) that she had become sick as "punishment," because she had dared to dance with that gallant ladies' man, Lucio Blanco.[30]

All in all, the general received an excellent report card from the populace on both sides of the river, especially for a revolutionary who vowed to redistribute the wealth in his domain.

Lucio Blanco remembered his commitment to the poor. Soon after the fall of Matamoros, Johnson, the U.S. consul, had said: ". . . the Constitutionalist program has the approval of the masses of Mexico. They intend to divide up the big estates among the people; so that the country will be changed from one of a few wealthy landlords and a great many homeless and ignorant peons to one of small

Lucio Blanco. Courtesy of the Hidalgo County Historical Society.

farmers. They believe that the Mexicans have been kept in ignorance long enough, and that conditions in Mexico will never improve until the people are given a chance to become educated.[31]

Blanco had "liberated" peons from debts and landlessness en route to Matamoros, and now he intended to lay the cornerstone of national agrarian reform. On July 27, 1913, he formed a special commission of ten, including his adjutant, Francisco Múgica, and chaired by Francisco Madero's former assistant commissioner of public works, and charged them to develop a plan for redistribution to benefit the poor and land-starved *campesinos*. Within a month the commission had designed a blueprint.[32]

Just eight miles upriver from Matamoros Félix Díaz owned a massive hacienda called Los Borregos, which adjoined the Rio Grande. Its 75,000 acres were said to be worth half a million dollars in gold. Now that he had deposed the Félix Díaz clique in Matamoros (Díaz himself had by this time lost out to Huerta in the capital), Blanco eyed Los Borregos as a symbol for his land-reform intentions. With that in mind, he and his commission determined to formally divide up the hacienda among his soldiers, especially those from the state of Tamaulipas, along with ordinary campesinos, including those who had worked as sharecroppers, tenant farmers, and peons on the huge property.[33]

Celebratory preparations for the land division were elaborate; this was ritual at its finest. Individual holdings were to be measured by boundary lines running perpendicular to the Rio Grande; this would insure that each recipient received property *de abajo* (irrigable land along the river) for sowing corn and *de arriba* (land above the river suitable for dry farming) on which to plant cotton. However, the land was not free; recipients would pay one-twentieth of the purchase price in the first year and the balance over the next two decades.[34] Unfortunately, the record has not yet yielded to historians the precise purchase price, nor is it known where the payments went, if they were ever realized at all.

Applicants received parcels in accordance with the size of their families. Octavio Gobea, for example, who had lived on the property for sixteen years, acquired fifty-five hectares (135.9 acres) for himself,

All those applying for land were required to fill out a questionnaire such as this one filed by Francisco Hernández y Coronado.

his wife, and four children.[35] All the campesinos completed questionnaires concerning their eligibility, and the few questionnaires that remain as examples suggest the nature of distribution and character of the recipients. For instance, Francisco Hernández y Coronado, was a native of Matamoros and a thirty-three-year-old married farmer with four daughters. He already possessed some fifteen to twenty acres of property and had sufficient food on hand to last at least until the next crop. In other words, Hernández did not plead hunger when completing the request form. He planted cotton, corn, and beans, the majority on irrigated land, and therefore had at least one marketable crop. Hernández said he not only lived on and worked land at his rancho called Gutiérrez, but also cultivated property in Los Borregos, so he quite possibly already owned a modest rancho. He could have been either a sharecropper at Los Borregos or had tenant arrangements; or he might have actually owned a small piece of land within the hacienda—such conditions were not uncommon in Mexico. Finally, Hernández acknowledged that he had been despoiled of no land, nor was he a soldier serving the cause. There is no way of knowing whether or not Hernández was typical of those chosen to receive titled land from Los Borregos; all that we can confirm is that he received thirteen hectares.[36]

The day of distribution was Saturday afternoon, August 30, 1913; Blanco was determined to make it a banner day. The Agrarian Commission in charge of the division of lands issued formal invitations to citizens of both Matamoros and Brownsville, journalists and photographers included. Robert Runyon stood among the special guests and with his camera recorded for posterity the revolution's land-reform program in action. Blanco assembled the soldiers of his brigade for the occasion, and late in the afternoon the martial music and speechmaking began.

"Finally, after much effort, three years of war and sacrifice, the Revolution is beginning to orient itself toward the resolution of one of the great problems that constitutes, without doubt, the principal core of prosperity in our country: the equal distribution of land," Blanco began. He then argued that control of the country by a few large landowners under government protection reduced the national wealth and destroyed motivation among the common people. He scored the dictatorship ousted by the Madero rebellion and assured his listeners that rights usurped from humble Mexicans would now be returned to them. He offered soldiers of the revolution and their families titles to land, so that after the struggle they might return to a rewarding farming life. After these brief remarks he began the redistribution.[37]

At a rustic table, its legs firmly dug into rich soil and draped with a colorful serape from his native Coahuila, Lucio Blanco solemnly signed property titles and bestowed them on the new owners. Florentino Izaguirre received the first grant. The title document itself carried the emblem of the moment: a large plot of farmland divided by a deep furrow in which rested an up-to-date plow. In the background, mountains and the sun, which beamed "1910" and, slightly lower, "1913." In front of this bucolic scene, crossed rifles lay against two

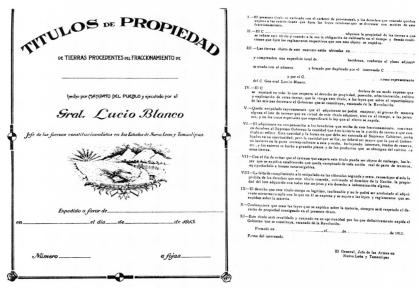

Modelo de los Títulos de Propiedad de las repartidas por el general Blanco en agosto de 1914, reparto suspendido por órdenes de la Primera Jefatura de la Revolución Constitucionalista.

A property title like those given to successful applicants.

cut stalks of corn.[38] Informed of the land distribution implemented outside Matamoros, Jean Jaures, the great French socialist, remarked to the Paris press: "Now I know why they are fighting in Mexico."[39] Texas newspapers reported the redistribution without editorial comment.

But the reaction of Venustiano Carranza to the redistribution was quite different. Blanco had not consulted with the chief of the Constitutionalists about any land-reform project. Furthermore, Carranza believed that such distribution was premature. Indeed, another year and a half passed before Carranza found it propitious to announce an agrarian program of his own. As unhappy as he was with the actions of his subordinate, Carranza dared not deprive Blanco of his triumph at Matamoros. Instead he promoted Blanco to brigadier general and at the same time named General Pablo González to command the entire Army of the Northeast (Coahuila, Tamaulipas and Nuevo León), making Blanco his subordinate, a status that Blanco could not long countenance.

An enraged Lucio Blanco obeyed Carranza's order but refused to fulfill his duties under González, a favorite ploy used by wary and disgruntled Spanish administrators during Mexico's colonial experience. Blanco simply would not fight for González. Instead, he could frequently be seen riding a magnificent horse around Matamoros, seated on a leopard-skin saddle blanket and brandishing a gold-headed riding crop. Certainly, he kept supplies moving through the city and on to Constitutionalist forces farther south. And he raised funds by forcing ranchers, both American and Mexican, to export their cattle to the United States while charging them a hefty tax for the privilege. Carranza only briefly tolerated Blanco's obstinacy and, in October 1913, transferred him to serve far away under Alvaro Obregón on the country's west coast.[40]

The revolutionaries relentlessly pressed toward the capital at Mexico City, and with a boost from the Wilson administration, which landed Marines and sailors at Veracruz to interdict the federal government's supply route, they finally forced Victoriano Huerta into exile in July 1914. Then the victors began to argue among themselves over the succession. Soon enough the fissures produced armed con-

flict, and Blanco broke with the Constitutionalists to join another faction. Obregón caught up with the defector in the fall of 1916. Trials for disobedience and usurpation of authority resulted in Blanco's exile in the United States. Then in 1919, when Carranza, who had become president of Mexico, faced a rebellious threat from his former ally, Obregón, the president engaged Blanco as an aide. However, Carranza soon lost his power struggle with Obregón, and Blanco was once again forced into exile. From tactical positions in Laredo and San Antonio, Blanco staged several raids across the border against Obregón, Mexico's new president. In June 1922 Blanco unsuspectingly attended a party in Laredo. Someone at the festivities drugged him, carried his limp form to Mexico (undoubtedly with accomplices), murdered him, and dumped his corpse into the Rio Grande. Some people assumed Obregón's participation in the scheme, perhaps with U.S. complicity, but proof has yet to be established. Despite such an ignoble ending to his life, Lucio Blanco has emerged as a genuine hero of the Mexican Revolution.[41]

Lucio Blanco initiated the land reform which is the hallmark of the Mexican Revolution. Zapata probably had earlier returned despoiled land to some followers, and some casual conversation has it that a minor redistribution occurred in Sonora prior to that at Los Borregos. But Blanco is the acknowledged initiator of his country's agrarian program. His adjutant, Francisco Múgica, who accompanied him at the Hacienda de los Borregos, later wrote the agrarian reform provision incorporated into the Mexican Constitution of 1917, which stands today. Whether the reform program as envisioned by Blanco has been instituted is a subject of debate. Félix Díaz may have lost Los Borregos to the reform, but in 1927, from exile in New Orleans, he still legally defended other property he owned downriver, east of Matamoros.[42] Furthermore, Blanco's ideals have been shaped into a potent political tool wielded by the powerful to protect their interests in the name of public peace.

In another and perhaps even more important way, events at Los Borregos may have influenced the flow of the great revolution itself. In mid-1913, just as Blanco approached Matamoros, the Wilson administration in Washington, D.C., found itself in a quandary over its Mexico policy. Armed intervention remained publicly out of the question, although privately the U.S. military, some politicians, and representatives of big business talked about the possibility. The problem concerned not only getting rid of the stubborn Victoriano Huerta, who refused to kowtow to the United States, but to find a replacement who would be palatable to U.S. political and economic interests.

Americans, who owned enormous tracts in most every part of Mexico, certainly did not favor a radical land reformer. That is what made them fret about Villa and Zapata. When Lucio Blanco divided up Los Borregos, it did not go uncriticized among Americans with business dealings in Mexico. However, when Carranza chastised Blanco for his inopportune and self-sponsored land-reform program, policymaking Americans apparently took notice. Some historians, such as John Hart, have concluded that it was precisely at this juncture that the U.S. government decided to back the moderate reformist Carranza and to frustrate the more radical intentions of populist leaders.[43] With U.S. assistance, Carranza was able to defeat his adversaries and to bend the struggle in ways which better suited U.S. interests.

It is doubtful that Robert Runyon realized any of this when he took his photographs at Los Borregos. As his later political career proved, he resolutely defended private property; according to his son, Delbert, he never would have approved of confiscation. Yet he appreciated history in the making. So when his wife's brother-in-law, who had joined the Constitutionalists, told him that Blanco needed a photographer to record the redistribution of hacienda lands, Runyon eagerly obliged. Personal feelings aside, he knew a great moment when he saw it, especially through the lens of his camera.

Matamoros remained a *carrancista* stronghold for the rest of the Mexican Revolution. However, across the river in Brownsville no such unanimity existed. Various contenders for power in Mexico plotted strategy from the U.S. side of the line, and American merchants eagerly supplied whatever faction with war matériel. Repercussions of Carranza's split with Pancho Villa in late 1914 reverberated in Brownsville, and the ambiance intensified as the populace drew sides. So much so that the state district judge had to issue a statement urging restraint:

At this particular time, all along this border and particularly here in Brownsville and Cameron County, it becomes necessary that our citizenship should arise to the occasion and gird on the armor of true manhood with a view of restoring harmony and good will, instead of sowing the seed of discord and strife, and while we sympathize with that war stricken country, yet it is an affair with which, as a people, we have nothing to do, and our citizens should exercise caution and prudence in expressing their views on the subject. I am told that many of the people of Brownsville have "lined up" with one or the other of the factions in Mexico and have become strong partisans of one side or the other, and that this partisan feeling runs nearly as high on this side of the river as on the other side. Such a condition is deplorable and should not be encouraged, for it cannot possibly produce any good, but much harm may result from it. We have enough bickering and discord amongst ourselves, without borrowing trouble from another country, with whose affairs we ought not to meddle, and in my judgment, the least partisanship displayed by us for either faction, the better it will be for all concerned. . . .[44]

Well said, perhaps, but as Villa's army approached Matamoros, it openly recruited soldiers and solicited supplies from U.S. territory, and by the spring of 1915 some 7,000 *villistas* under Generals José Rodríguez and Absaul Navarro stood before the terrorized city. But the defense, directed by Nafarrate, was ready; sixteen machine guns and 1,000 hand grenades proved their worth against the *villista* cavalry charge, and an airplane piloted by an American mercenary which was to bomb Matamoros never did materialize. When *villistas* crossed to the U.S. side of the river to gain a better enfilade on Matamoros, Nafarrate told Consul Johnson to resolve the problem or he would be forced to rake U.S. territory with machine guns. Soon after, U.S. soldiers drove the *villistas* back into Mexico.[45]

On April 13 the *carrancistas* took the offensive; they first blunted their enemy's artillery barrage and then drove their adversary from the field in utter defeat. Coupled with the spectacular victories over

Villa himself about the same time in central Mexico, the successful defense of Matamoros provided Carranza with the military impetus that he needed for his Constitutionalist movement to triumph.[46] However, diplomatic success still eluded Venustiano Carranza. Specifically, he still lacked the official recognition of the United States, but, as we shall see in the following chapter, the astute and tough-minded leader had conceived plans about how that might be accomplished.

Before the deluge, and in one of the first of thousands of photographs that Runyon took in Matamoros, the army troops of Mexico's dictator Porfirio Díaz parade down Sixth Street (the main street) at the city's zócalo. The Palacio Municipal is the first building from the left and the Plaza de Armas is at the right. The carriages belonged to the city's taxi system. Notably, only a sparse crowd of spectators witnessed the ceremony. Courtesy of the Barker Texas History Center.

Mexico's internationally famed rural police force, the Rurales, was reorganized and expanded by Francisco Madero's victorious government during the first phase of the revolution. Many considered these Rurales the best constabulary in the world—even better than the Texas Rangers. Dressed in their bolero jackets and leg-hugging pants with an ornate silver strip on the outer seam, and distinguished by their wide-brimmed sombreros, they cut a handsome figure, especially when on parade, like this crack troop organized in Matamoros. This group fought for the Victoriano Huerta regime against the Constitutionalists and was scattered in the battle for the city in 1913. Courtesy of the Barker Texas History Center.

As the Constitutionalists approached, Matamoros braced itself. Defenders tossed up barricades across the major streets of the city: logs, railroad ties, sandbags, stones, and any other debris they could lay their hands on. Such barricades were meant to break the cavalry charges of the enemy. On the fringes of the city they dug trenches for the infantry and in front of them erected barbed wire fences which they then electrified. Dynamite sticks were laid as mines. Much of the defense was jerry-rigged but proved to be lethal. Courtesy of the Barker Texas History Center.

Fewer than fifty federal soldiers garrisoned Matamoros at the time of the impending attack. They were like these men; they looked fine in their uniforms, but most were young fellows who lacked military training. Reports that reinforcements were on the way emanated from Mexico City and other major military concentrations, but none ever arrived, and the federals never made any real attempt to retake the city. Courtesy of the Barker Texas History Center.

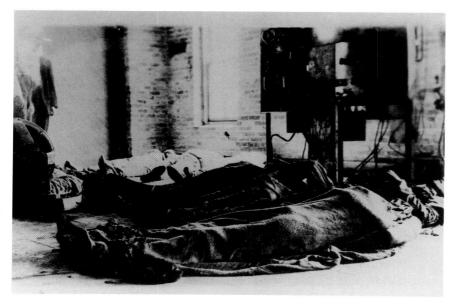

The Constitutionalists struck Matamoros the morning of June 3, 1913. By all accounts, most of them by citizens of Brownsville who watched the carnage from the tops of hotels and railroad cars on their side of the river, the battle everywhere was ferocious. A major fight centered on the city's electric power plant, located on the Rio Grande just west of the main population center. For five or six hours the federals held the plant against withering attacks by the enemy. There was heroism on both sides. Finally, the defenders retreated in bloody defeat to the U.S. side of the line. Runyon, among the first on the scene when the fighting subsided, photographed some of the ugly results. Courtesy of the Hidalgo County Historical Museum.

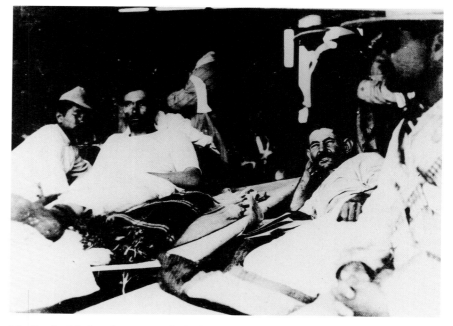

Medical aid for the wounded, from both the American Red Cross and private physicians with volunteer help, arrived as soon as conditions permitted. The victors set up a hospital in the power plant, not only one of the city's more durable buildings but the scene of their most crucial encounter. Courtesy of the Hidalgo County Historical Museum.

MEXICAN TROOPS
MARCHING.
© R RUNYON.

The federals, their situation hopeless, surrendered the city on the morning of June 4. Many escaped to Brownsville; others fled south. But as the Constitutionalists who had been held in reserve on the fringes of town rode toward the main plaza, they were unopposed. All day long they poured into Brownsville, and Runyon was there to capture their spirited arrival on film. Courtesy of the Barker Texas History Center.

LUGAR DONDE FUERON EJECUTADOS 19 JOBENES
VOLUNTARIOS EL DIA 4 DE JUNIO 1913. POR LAS
FUERZAS CARRANCISTAS. H. MATAMOROS.
⟨PROPIEDAD ARTISTICA ASEGURADA⟩

Among those executed were nineteen young boys who had been hustled into the defense of their families and the city. The rebel commander, Lucio Blanco, later blamed the executions on subordinates. Blanco said he had ordered only the execution of a few federals who had raised the white flag of surrender and then fired upon his soldiers who approached them. But Blanco's disclaimer was then and still is taken with much skepticism. Runyon took this picture which was then pirated for sale by a Mexican entrepreneur—or the other way around. Courtesy of the Barker Texas History Center.

The victors showed only limited mercy to the vanquished. And in concert with the tragedies which inevitably accompany these kinds of encounters, they mercilessly executed some thirty of the prisoners they captured. Here they executed twenty-three-year-old Antonio Echazaretta, who, as a volunteer himself who held the rank of colonel, headed up the contingent of volunteers who defended the city. Many Americans attended the execution, including the U.S. consul, Jesse H. Johnson. Note how the execution was staged for the "official" photographer, Robert Runyon. The victim was seated in strong sunlight to ensure a good photo record of the event. Courtesy of the Barker Texas History Center.

The afternoon of June 4 found survivors of the battle and others who had taken refuge in Brownsville back in Matamoros to assess the toll. It was quite high for such brief combat: more than one hundred dead and several hundred wounded. Because the defense included not only the regular army and the Rurales, but the local militia supported by volunteers, any number of families were touched by the horrors of the fighting. For days, people reported missing slowly filtered back into town. Meanwhile, bodies of the dead were burned on two huge pyres and the remains buried in common graves. The town itself escaped large-scale destruction, and Constitutionalist commanders controlled looting. Courtesy of the Barker Texas History Center.

Lucio Blanco was the well-educated, English-speaking son of a Coahuilan rancher who had supported Francisco Madero—the martyred chief of the Mexican Revolution—in his campaigns for free and fair elections. Moreover, Blanco possessed a strong liberal streak, even more so than Madero, especially when it came to helping the poor to obtain land and sustenance for their daily lives. Here he speaks informally with several of his followers; he seems to have been quite accessible to the people. Courtesy of the Hidalgo County Historical Museum.

Daily life, including the Matamoros taxi service, quickly returned to normal under Constitutionalist occupation. Blanco guaranteed foreign property against molestation, although he raised revenue by charging a heavy head tax on export cattle. He also planned to divide up large land holdings in the region (some of them foreign-owned) among poor and landless campesinos. Courtesy of the Barker Texas History Center.

Soldaderas—women soldiers—campaigned with the revolutionaries. Most cooked for and in other ways comforted the men, but some women actually participated in the fighting. In its June 5 edition, the *San Antonio Express* lauded four women who fought for Blanco at the Battle of Matamoros. Here several *soldaderas*, dressed in finery, carry the rifles with which they purportedly fought. Courtesy of the Barker Texas History Center.

Young boys, this one standing on a bale of hay to be photographed, also joined the rebels, more often as spies than as fighters. They would casually infiltrate enemy positions before an attack and then report back on military conditions to be faced. They also served as messengers and smugglers. At times they carried poignant messages from a rebel to relatives in a town about to be assaulted. Courtesy of the Barker Texas History Center.

To emphasize the nature of their cause and as recruiting strategy, Blanco's officers distributed money to the city's poor. Some Constitutionalists, in other places, actually issued their own currency in order to control the regional economy, but this did not occur around Matamoros. The distribution of cash seems to have been more symbolic than real; Blanco needed money to buy weapons, and other rebels did not hesitate to line their pockets with the booty of war. Courtesy of the Barker Texas History Center.

Blanco enjoyed aggressive and able assistants, including his chief of staff Major Francisco José Múgica, who later drafted the famed agrarian plank to the nation's new Constitution of 1917. Lt. Col. Daniel Rios Zertuche, a doctor who had attended medical school in Atlanta, served as the main interpreter for the unit. These advisors not only abetted Blanco's military campaigns but his reform program. Together they organized an agrarian commission dedicated to getting land and resources into the hands of needy campesinos. In short, they meant to elevate the Mexican poor. As a start, they decided to confiscate and subdivide the large hacienda called Los Borregos, which belonged to Félix Díaz, nephew of the deposed dictator, Porfirio, and a major instigator in the coup which overthrew Madero. Runyon photographed this good-looking group for the *San Antonio Express*, which featured the picture on page one of its September 5, 1913, edition. Blanco is seated fifth from the left. Courtesy of the Barker Texas History Center.

By all accounts, Blanco lived it up while celebrating his victory at Matamoros. He sponsored Sunday luncheons for the businessmen of Brownsville and sumptuous *bailes* for notables from both sides of the border, including the Mexican family of Runyon's future wife. Here the rebel commander stands outside of his favorite touring car, although he apparently preferred to be seen riding his splendid horse through the streets of Matamoros. Courtesy of the Barker Texas History Center.

With this photograph, Runyon inscribed in history one of the momentous events of the Mexican Revolution: the inauguration of a land reform program, which is still the hallmark of the "continuing revolution." In a sumptuous ceremony, attended by regional dignitaries from both sides of the river, Blanco and his staff first surveyed (note the surveying instrument to the right) and then delivered parcels of Los Borregos to eleven campesinos who had worked the property for Félix Díaz. Blanco is seen signing the ownership papers on a table covered by a famous Saltillo serape, trademark of his home state. Courtesy of the Barker Texas History Center.

The recipients of land received parcels in accordance with the size of their families. For example, Octavio Gobea (unidentified in the photo) obtained title for seventy-five acres for his family of six. Some of the acreage fronted the Rio Grande and was therefore irrigable. In fact, all of the farmers got some land which could be irrigated, and the rest remained good for dry farming. Gobea had worked on Los Borregos for sixteen years, probably as a sharecropper or tenant farmer. Not all of these campesinos were desperately poor; some possessed plots elsewhere or otherwise managed additional income. But, in essence, they were typical subsistence farmers. Courtesy of the Barker Texas History Center.

By the time of this photo in the fall of 1913, Runyon and Blanco had parted company. Blanco's aggressive land-reform program had angered his superior, the Constitutionalist chief Venustiano Carranza, who first promoted Blanco to general as compensation for his victory at Matamoros and then transferred him to the west coast of Mexico for his ambitious and unapproved agrarian schemes. Runyon then followed the Constitutionalists through their important victories in Victoria, the capital of Tamaulipas, and on to Monterrey, the major city in Mexico's entire northeast. To carry ammunition and other war supplies on campaign toward Victoria, the Constitutionalists commandeered a small fleet of autos and hired some Americans to drive them. Runyon caught them taking a coffee break. Courtesy of the Barker Texas History Center.

CARRANZA'S SOLDIERS COOKING DINNER.

170

As they advanced over enormous distances, the Constitutionalists foraged for their food. As this was cattle country, the troops rarely lacked for *carne asada* cooked over mesquite fires. *Soldaderas* normally did the actual cooking. Courtesy of the Barker Texas History Center.

Concerned by Lucio Blanco's aggressive independence, the chief of the Constitutionalist revolution, Venustiano Carranza (left), ordered Blanco to the west coast of Mexico and turned the eastern campaign over to Blanco's rival, General Pablo González. Blanco later split with his commander-in-chief, was soon tried by the victorious *carrancistas* for treason, and was exiled to the United States, where in 1922 he was kidnapped and murdered, possibly on dictates from Mexico City. Courtesy of the Barker Texas History Center.

2. Runyon Records the Mexican Revolution

1. For examples see John Mason Hart, *Revolutionary Mexico: The Coming and Process of the Mexican Revolution* and Alan Knight, *The Mexican Revolution*.

2. For one among many published overviews of the tangled neutrality issues see Coerver and Hall, *Texas and the Mexican Revolution*.

3. Rodolfo Rocha, "The Influence of the Mexican Revolution on the Mexico-Texas Border, 1910–1916," pp. 68–69.

4. Ibid., p. 70.

5. Ibid., pp. 92, 95–96.

6. Ibid., pp. 96–97.

7. Coerver and Hall, *Texas and the Mexican Revolution*, p. 58.

8. Governor Colquitt's disputes with the federal government are well researched and described in ibid.

9. Ibid., pp. 58–59.

10. Ibid., p. 80.

11. Much has been written on Wilsonian diplomacy during this period. For example see Mark T. Gilderhus, *Diplomacy and Revolution: U.S.–Mexican Relations under Wilson and Carranza*.

12. Biographical details on Lucio Blanco are from Alfonso F. Sapia-Bosch, "The Role of Lucio Blanco in the Mexican Revolution, 1913–1922," pp. 1–3; and Armando de María y Campos, *La Vida del General Lucio Blanco*.

13. Sapia-Bosch, "The Role of Lucio Blanco," pp. 4–6, 9–11.

14. Ibid., pp. 17–19.

15. Stambaugh and Stambaugh, *The Lower Rio Grande Valley of Texas*, pp. 208–209.

16. Ibid.

17. Ibid., p. 209; Rocha, "The Influence of the Mexican Revolution," pp. 147–148; *Brownsville Herald*, May 30, 1913.

18. John C. Rayburn and Virginia Kemp Rayburn, eds., *Century of Conflict: Incidents in the Lives of William Neale and William A. Neale, Early Settlers in Texas*, p. 149; *San Antonio Light*, June 1, 1913; *Brownsville Herald*, May 14, 1913. For military details concerning the Battle of Matamoros, see Ciro R. de la Garza Treviño, *La Revolución mexicana en el Estado de Tamaulipas*, pp. 175–179.

19. Rayburn and Rayburn, *Century of Conflict*, p. 150.

20. Ibid., pp. 150–151.

21. Ibid.

22. *San Antonio Light*, June 4, 1913; *Brownsville Herald*, June 3, 1917, June 7, 1917.

23. J. L. Allhands, *Gringo Builders*, pp. 264–265; Sapia-Bosch, "The Role of Lucio Blanco," p. 35.

24. *Brownsville Herald*, Aug. 29, 1913.

25. Stambaugh and Stambaugh, *The Lower Rio Grande Valley*, p. 209; Garza Treviño, *Tamaulipas*; *Brownsville Herald*, June 9, 1913.

26. Rocha, "The Influence of the Mexican Revolution," pp. 148–149; María y Campos, *Vida del General Lucio Blanco*, p. 67; Sapia-Bosch, "The Role of Lucio Blanco," pp. 43–45; Garza Treviño, *Tamaulipas*, p. 178.

27. *Brownsville Herald*, June 16, 1913.

28. Ibid., July 3, 1913.

29. Ibid., June 7, 1913.

30. Interview, Runyon family reunion, Austin, Oct. 20, 1989.

31. *Brownsville Herald*, July 3, 1913.

32. Ibid., July 28, 1913.

33. The story of the redistribution of Los Borregos is best told in María y Campos, *Vida del General Lucio Blanco*, pp. 55–65. Also see Sapia-Bosch, "The Role of Lucio Blanco," pp. 49–55.

34. *Brownsville Herald*, Sept. 1, 1913.

35. Ibid., p. 35.

36. María y Campos, *Vida del General Lucio Blanco*, pp. 56–57.

37. Ibid., pp. 58–62.

38. Ibid., p. 61.

39. Ibid., p. 65.

40. Sapia-Bosch, "The Role of Lucio Blanco," pp. 59–60.

41. Ibid., pp. 184–259.

42. Record of Alien Ownership, 1: 35, vault, Cameron County Clerk's Office, Brownsville.

43. Hart, *Revolutionary Mexico*, p. 281.

44. Rocha, "The Influence of the Mexican Revolution," p. 228.

45. Canseco, *Matamoros*, pp. 212–214.

46. Rocha, "The Influence of the Mexican Revolution," pp. 210–211; and José Raul Canseco Botello, *Historia de Matamoros*, pp. 216–217.

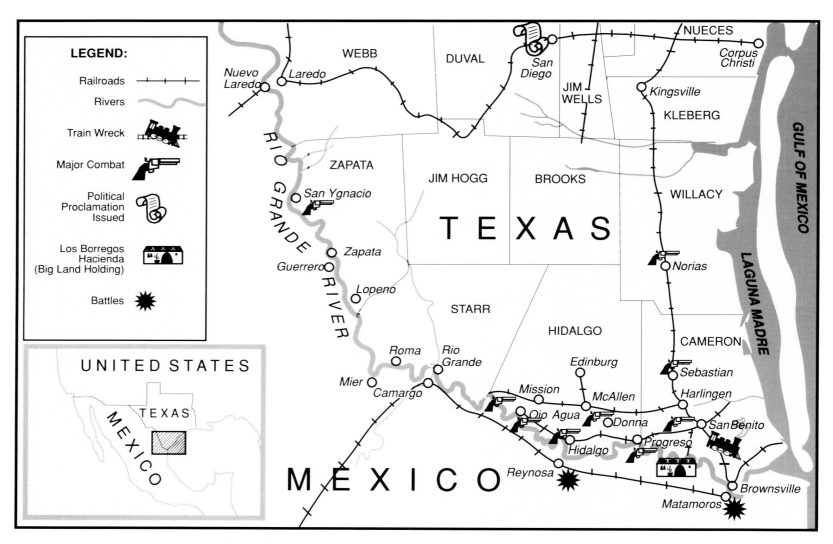

LEGEND:

Railroads ┤┤┤┤┤

Rivers

Train Wreck

Major Combat

Political Proclamation Issued

Los Borregos Hacienda (Big Land Holding)

Battles

UNITED STATES

TEXAS

MEXICO

NUECES

Corpus Christi

WEBB

DUVAL

San Diego

JIM WELLS

Kingsville

KLEBERG

Nuevo Laredo

Laredo

RIO GRANDE RIVER

ZAPATA

JIM HOGG

BROOKS

WILLACY

T E X A S

San Ygnacio

Zapata

Guerrero

Lopeno

STARR

Norias

GULF OF MEXICO

LAGUNA MADRE

HIDALGO

CAMERON

Roma

Rio Grande

Edinburg

Sebastian

Mier

Camargo

Mission

McAllen

Harlingen

Ojo Agua

Donna

Progreso

San Benito

Hidalgo

M E X I C O

Reynosa

Brownsville

Matamoros

LOWER RIO GRANDE VALLEY: 1913-1916

3. Rebellion and Retaliation

Border raiding is endemic to the Lower Rio Grande. Far from an obstacle, there the river has offered opportunity and sanctuary to those who understood how to use the international boundary to their advantage. Much of the interchange involved perfectly legal trade and commerce, but smuggling and cattle rustling also occurred. In fact, criminal and legitimate enterprise intermingled in the region—which was largely a no man's land—until well into this century. Banditry, bold killings, robberies, political plotting, and similar activities thrived in an atmosphere which suited businessmen, officeholders, ex-convicts, escaped prisoners, adventurers, army deserters, and all sorts of desperadoes. This dynamic story has yet to find a teller to do justice to all its fascinating details.[1]

The outbreak of the Mexican Revolution only created more turmoil in the area. Rebels south of the river needed supplies; business concerns to the north proved anxious to comply, at a good price. Payment was the problem. Impecunious campesinos who made up the bulk of the disparate rebel units south of the international line had no funds with which to purchase war goods. To get what they needed, they ransomed and confiscated where they could, and raided and looted elsewhere. Naturally, these activities spilled back and forth across the border, even more so because many who joined the revolution were Mexicans or Mexican Americans who lived on the U.S. side of the river. Accustomed to crossing the line at will, they knew the territory on both sides. So did a good many Anglo-Americans from the region who had long engaged in informal business exchanges and friendships with Mexicans on the other side. The advent of revolution created new opportunities for these people along with a rash of troubles.

As the revolution gathered momentum, the U.S. government as well as Texas authorities tried to regulate the border trade with troops, militia, and other law enforcement personnel. The federal government had diplomatic responsibilities to fulfill toward Mexico, a friendly neighbor. Under its neutrality statutes, the United States was obligated to prevent war matériel and recruits from reaching the rebels from the United States. The task proved impossible, not only because the army was too small and inefficient to do any such job at the time, but because so many good American capitalists yearned to profit from Mexico's ordeal. When the army proved incapable of protecting Texans from Mexican raiding parties as well as from bullets which inevitably zinged across the frontier when the fighting engulfed Mexican border towns, Texas governor Oscar B. Colquitt called out the state militia and the famed Texas Rangers to restore order. Of course, they could not. In fact, friction between them and the federal forces only exacerbated the dilemma.[2]

These agitated conditions crested in the spring of 1915, when authorities in the Lower Rio Grande uncovered a sensational plot to ignite a far-reaching racial war in the United States. The goals were outlined in a so-called Plan de San Diego, named after the little Texas town somewhat over one hundred miles northwest of Brownsville on the rail line from Corpus Christi to Laredo. Bureau of Investigation agents found the plan among documents they recovered from Basilio Ramos, Jr., a Mexican national. Ramos had meddled in his country's politics since the days of the old dictatorship and was apparently recruiting on behalf of the plan around McAllen when arrested in January 1915. Four months later federal authorities in Brownsville charged him with conspiring to steal "certain property of the United States of America . . . , to wit, the states of Texas, Oklahoma, New Mexico, Arizona, Colorado and California . . . ."[3]

This extraordinary Plan de San Diego called for a general uprising of Mexican Americans, blacks, and Japanese on February 20, 1915, to proclaim the independence of five states: California, Colorado, New Mexico, Arizona, and Texas. The Liberating Army of Races and Peoples would fight under a red-and-white banner emblazoned with the motto "Equality and Independence." In the process, all Anglo males over sixteen years would be killed. Somehow all of this would eventually lead to the abolition of racial hatred and the founding of a new society based in "universal love."

As the plan moved toward triumph, blacks would be given six states contiguous to the region encompassed by the aforementioned states in order to establish their own republic; it would then constitute a buffer between the remnant of the United States of America and the new country carved from America's former southwest territories. American Indians would also be accommodated in the scheme. No assistance toward these rambunctious ends would be solicited from Mexico, but the directorate of the enterprise might later request annexation by Mexico.

February 20 came and went without any undue excitement in the Valley. A revised Plan de San Diego soon appeared as a Manifesto to the Oppressed Peoples of America. It reaffirmed the goals of the original plan, but now heralded a social revolution. It aimed to create a Social Republic of Texas, made up of Arizona, New Mexico, California, Colorado, Nevada, and Utah. But no linkage between the authors of the original plan and its revision has been established, if any ever existed. However, this mattered little to U.S. authorities. Neither plan had whipped up any support, so the government reduced Ramos's bail bond from $5,000 to $100, which he promptly made and then jumped into the security of Mexico. Texas Ranger captain J. J. Sanders reported from San Benito to his superiors on

Recruitment poster for the Plan de San Diego.

March 1 that revolutionaries were holding meetings in the Valley, "causing considerable uneasiness among white people."[4] Shortly thereafter, all hell broke loose along the Lower Rio Grande.[5] American and Mexican farmers working the region began to report the daily loss of cattle, saddles, and other equipment in May 1915. U.S. Army units investigated but encountered only frustration. It was common for American cattlemen to buy cattle known to be stolen in Mexico for half the local market price, but those who benefited from the practice were not about to reveal their sources to authorities.[6]

Nonetheless, while such activities certainly were not foreign to the district, these latest raids seemed to be especially well orchestrated by large groups, and their growing intensity concerned the residents. Farmers spotted a band of Mexicans, maybe twenty or thirty men, near Sebastian, thirty miles north of Brownsville, but a posse of deputy sheriffs and "interested citizens" never could catch up with them. On July 12 eleven heavily armed Mexicans forced the store owner at Lyford, some forty miles north of Brownsville, to supply them with food and ammunition, and five days later the raiders purportedly killed a young American in the area. That same week bandits burned a St. Louis, Brownsville and Mexico Railway bridge outside Sebastian and then raided a ranch at Los Indios, where they killed a Mexican who apparently worked there. Then came a letter written in Spanish which threatened an attack on Brownsville itself.[7] These raiders obviously had more than cattle rustling on their minds, and it did not take long for a reaction to set in.

Society in the Lower Rio Grande had a long time been held in place by a patronal system, but the law often came at the point of a pistol or at the end of a rope. For most Anglos who ruled the region, there were "good" Mexicans and "bad" ones, and at times Anglos distinguished extremely arbitrarily between the two.[8] So it was not entirely unexpected that about ten o'clock on the night of July 25, an automobile intercepted Deputy Sheriffs Frank Carr and Daniel Hinojosa, who were transporting a prisoner, Adolfo Muñoz, from San Benito to the county jail at Brownsville. The intruders implicated Muñoz in the robbery and murder of a recluse merchant,

and as the press reported it, the prisoner was later "found dangling at the end of a rope tied to the limb of a mesquite tree. . . . Life was extinct."[9] They accused him of theft and of allegedly trying to rape a young girl from the area, and then they hanged and shot him. Only five days earlier deputy sheriffs had killed the Manríquez brothers, Lorenzo and Gorgonio, at Mercedes. The brothers had been denounced as robbers, and the sheriffs later explained that they had resisted arrest. These events in calmer times might have avoided public notice, but revolution raging just below the border and the radicalized Plan of San Diego had strained nerves.[10]

Newspapers extolled the law enforcers. Outside the town of Mercedes, mounted U.S. Customs inspector J. D. White killed an individual who allegedly threatened his life. "Like a flash, White whipped out his revolver and this would-be assassin bit the dust. The man died from three shots, all well directed." The paper then noted that farmers and townspeople had organized to defend themselves against raiders, "and will administer swift justice to any thief caught."[11] When Rangers killed three "bandits" near Cameron City, the press reported, "The battle lasted hardly five seconds . . . . One man had 17 holes in his body. The bodies were left where they lay."[12]

The raiders aimed to cut communications in the Valley by burning bridges and cutting telegraph wires. They also set up some treacherous mantraps by stretching wires at night at head height along roads that paralleled railroad tracks. A motorist riding in an open car who struck the wires might have been decapitated. At least, that was the purpose of the trap. Automobiles were racing around the countryside as officials, authorized and others, tried to run down the raiders. Citizens of Sebastian formed a Law and Order League to enforce the peace, and when army units clashed with twenty-five to fifty rebels near San Benito, more than fifty automobiles loaded with citizens of the Valley armed to the teeth responded, demanding reprisals.[13]

August brought U.S. Army reinforcements and additional Texas Rangers to the fray, but by that time the marauders were striking ever more deeply into the area, even to that great symbol of Anglo domination, the sprawling Kenedy-King Ranch itself. On August 8, some sixty raiders attacked the Las Norias flag station on the great landholding, about seventy miles north of Brownsville along the St. Louis, Brownsville and Mexico Railway. The attackers apparently did not realize that elements of the Eighth U.S. Cavalry, state militiamen, and ten Texas Rangers had received reports of bandit activity in the area and were on the lookout for the brigands. While the majority of lawmen searched the prickly mesquite brush for their quarry, they left a military detachment at Las Norias, and the raiders ran smack into it.[14]

J. L. Allhands recounts the affair in his memoirs, decidedly from his point of view but capturing the flavor of the times:

> With the spread of Mexican terror the situation at the headquarters of the King properties in Willacy, Cameron, Hidalgo, Starr and Kenedy counties, known as Norias, and situated seven miles south of Armstrong, became acute. It meant constant watch with a mere handful of men to guard their headquarters. That little guard consisted of ranch foreman Frank Martin, Marcus Hines, Gordon Hill, Joe Taylor, a carpenter by the name of George Forbes, Albert, the colored cook, and eight soldiers of the Twelfth Cavalry.
>
> During this intense campaign Sam Robertson and vigilantes [self-appointed lawmen] Charles and Tom Armstrong, the sheriff of Willacy County and two deputies, together with three of Armstrong's trusted vaqueros, had been out combing the brush. Hours had passed without an iota of luck. [They had encountered no suspects.] It was Sunday evening when they had just returned and had sat down to supper. Black coffee had scarcely been poured when the telephone began to ring urgently, and the anxious, excited voice of Albert, the cook, gave them a wallop when he informed Charles Armstrong that all the Mexicans on earth were firing at the back of his head (the telephone was attached to the side of the house, and Albert had ventured out to use it, naturally making a fine target). Forthwith, and like wild fire, the Armstrong party galloped to their aid. At the same time Caesar Kleberg, who had also received their urgent SOS, was rushing reinforcements from Santa

Gertrudis by special train. When the rescue parties arrived at the bullet-torn headquarters, they found that the besiegers had been routed, leaving behind four or five of their dead and a couple of wounded, while on the side of the ranch force, a Mexican woman had been slain and Frank Martin, Mr. Forbes, and two soldiers wounded.[15]

These events, plus the lynching at San Benito of a Mexican accused of horse stealing, "seemed to fan the flame to a point where jingo revolutionists freely talked of re-taking Texas from the *gringos*," Allhands continued. "Some of the border bandits wore white hat bands which bore 'Viva la Independencia de Texas' and 'Viva Villa.' On the other hand, this provoked the savage radical element to a pitch where there were many glaring abuses in retribution and threatenings to clear the Valley of Mexicans."[16] The *Laredo Times* weighed in with the observation that "the recent happenings in Brownsville country indicate that there is a serious surplus population there that needs eliminating."[17]

The raids and reprisals continued all through August and on into September. U.S. cavalry units proved to be prime targets, and when they patroled the banks of the Rio Grande, Mexicans might shoot at them from the other side. Large bands of raiding Mexicans also suffered heavy casualties, and atrocities characterized both sides. On September 1 some thirty Mexicans burned buildings at a pumping plant fourteen miles north of Brownsville and took four prisoners: two Anglos and two Mexicans. En route to the little farming village of Fresnos, they took an American farmer prisoner. The raiders executed two of the Anglos in an old riverbed outside the town, but spared the third at the behest of the two Mexican prisoners, apparently because he had tended to a wounded Mexican soldier after a previous battle around Matamoros.[18]

One atrocity compounded another. Mexicans surrounded Galveston Ranch about twenty-four miles west of Brownsville, on the night of September 13 and fired on nine soldiers sleeping there. They killed one soldier and wounded two others. U.S. Army major Edward Anderson of the Twelfth Cavalry said he was positive the raiders were locals and were probably working as farmhands in the neighborhood of the fight a few hours after it ended.[19] Earlier that day an army patrol had arrested five Mexicans living at the ranch and turned them over to authorities at San Benito. During the night deputy sheriffs took three of the prisoners out of jail and started toward Harlingen. The next day the three were found executed along the road.

Less than two weeks later the Mexicans took what some saw as their revenge. When he returned on patrol to the Saenz store at Progreso (Hidalgo County) on September 24, Lieutenant W. King of the Twenty-sixth U.S. Infantry discovered one private dead and another wounded. He summoned reinforcements, and for the next twenty-four hours skirmishes flared between the military and perhaps seventy-five Mexican adversaries. During a lull the Americans discovered that one of their members, Private Richard J. Johnson of Troop B, Twelfth Cavalry, was missing from the guard at the Progreso crossing of the Rio Grande. They soon understood what had happened: twenty-one-year-old Johnson of Mount Morris, New York, had been taken prisoner and dragged across the river, where his captors first cut off his ears, then his head, and carried them off as souvenirs. The soldier's remains were tossed into the river.[20]

Inexorably the war plague gained momentum, especially after the vigilante Law and Order Leagues began their wanton executions of Mexican-American suspects in the Valley. Toward the end of July, peace officers and prominent citizens from throughout the Lower Rio Grande had gathered at San Benito to coordinate tactics in suppressing the raiders. There they agreed to exact "summary punishment . . . upon any suspected bandits who may fall into their hands." San Benito's mayor then appointed every man in town between the ages of twenty-one and sixty to be special policemen.[21]

In September, fourteen Mexican Americans were shot to death near Donna and their bodies, most dressed in blue overalls and some wearing soft felt hats, were stretched out along a roadway as a warning to others. J. T. Canales, a prominent Brownsville lawyer, organized his own law enforcers, called Canales Scouts, to combat the raiders, while the political boss of Hidalgo County, Deodoro Guerra, personally led posses against the "invaders." The *San Antonio Express* wrote that peace officers in the Valley "used a swift and effective type of border justice which rapidly ran down fugitive Mexicans of bad records, who are accused of complication [complicity?] in raids of the past two weeks. If he [the Mexican] is slow to explain [his activities] his life is in danger. If he makes a threatening move, his life is forfeited."[22]

The Texas Rangers also contributed to the mayhem. There were only thirty-four of them officially in the force in 1915, but they certainly made their presence felt. Within two years, "appointments" had substantially bolstered the force. Cecilia Almaguer Rendón, a native of Brownsville, tells us what it was like to be an ordinary Mexican American settled in the Valley when the Rangers arrived at your home:

They sent many "rinches" [derisive term used by locals to mean Rangers] to the area where we lived because they thought we were helping the Mexican bandits. . . The bandits would come around and ask for food, and if you didn't give them any, they would take what was already prepared. But the bandits never came to our home because the "rinches" were nearby.

On one occasion the "rinches" apprehended my cousin Encarnación Garza right in our farm, because they thought he was a bandit. He had come from Kingsville to visit my mother, because she had raised him. . . . He said he would sleep outside because it was too hot indoors. It was summertime. We didn't want him to sleep outside, because we had heard talk the "rinches" were coming around, and didn't know when they would arrive. At about 2:30 a.m. the "rinches" came and the first thing they found was my cousin. They got him up just the way he was; he was in his underclothes. They didn't let him put on his shoes or anything. They put on handcuffs and made him stand in front of the car lights. One guarded him and others searched the place.[23]

Cecilia Rendón was only a small child when the Rangers, with guns drawn, forced their way into the home of her parents and conducted a rough search of the premises, took the family's tortillas and *pan dulce*, and then returned to their captive:

The "rinches" then put my cousin in the car and left. They took him to a cemetery about a block away, placed him in front of a cross and shot him dead. We heard the noise. They left him laying there. The following morning instead of going to work in the fields as usual, we went to the cemetery. Poor cousin, there he was, just laying there. It happened that he had fallen right on my grandfather's grave, although the "rinches" didn't know that. He was about twenty-one years old. We didn't put him in a box. We just wrapped him in a sheet and a blanket, dug a deep grave, and put him in it. Then we covered him up. . . .[24]

This is the way that it went with the "rinches" Cecilia Rendón says, "we were afraid to challenge them, because they were like big animals and they had guns . . . . There was no remedy but to pray to God that the "rinches" go away . . . ."[25]

What could be expected of the Rangers, who sang while on patrol:

O bury me not on the lone praire-ee
Where the wild coyotes will howl over me!
In a narrow grave just six by three
Where all the Mexkins ought to be![26]

To which the Mexicans responded in one of their typical *corridos:*

Come on you cowardly Rangers
No baby is up against you.
You want to meet your daddy?
I am Jacinto Treviño.

Come on, you treacherous Rangers;
Come get a taste of my lead.
Or did you think it was ham
Between two slices of bread.[27]

No doubt a good many Mexicans had it in for the Rangers. *Carrancista* soldiers entrenched on the Mexican side of the Rio Grande shouted across to U.S. cavalry patrols that they would not fire on American soldiers, but that they had every reason to shoot Texas Rangers along with county officials and others.[28] Walter Prescott Webb, the popular biographer of the Rangers and certainly not inimical to the constabulary, estimates that 500 to 5,000 Mexicans were killed in the Valley during this period, compared with 62 American civilians and 64 soldiers.[29]

Not all Valley justice was administered vigilante style. The courts also played their part in local endeavors to restore the peace. In the spring of 1916, a grand jury indicted thirty-four individuals, mostly for triple counts of murder. But only four of them were convicted, an indication of how loosely the official net had settled over the countryside. Of the four, two received sentences of fifteen years each, and one of these convictions was later overturned. Brownsville's legal executioners hanged the remaining two in the midst of considerable local excitement.[30]

The death toll recorded by the Rangers and others in this mishmash of largely unaccountable law enforcement will never be known. Two decades later residents were still finding skeletons with bullet holes in the skulls. Major General Frederick Funston, who commanded the army's Southern Department during the period, estimated that state and local authorities "did execute by hanging or shooting approximately three hundred suspected Mexicans on [the] American side of [the] river."[31]

How can all this hateful turmoil be explained? Naturally, multiple causation existed, but what made the epoch so explosive was that it occurred at a historical conjuncture. About the turn of the century, James Wells, who was the political boss in the Lower Rio Grande, along with other wealthy people of the region, such as Robert Kleberg, Richard King II, and Robert Driscoll, Sr., financed the St. Louis, Brownsville and Mexico Railway, which tied Brownsville to the Corpus Christi terminal of the Missouri-Pacific Railroad some 160 miles to the north. That railroad opened up economic exchange in the Valley and attracted from faraway thousands of farmers, a number of them quite well off, anxious to exploit the region's commercial agricultural potential with expensive irrigation systems, the latest dry-farming techniques, and modern refrigerated railroad cars. South Texas had a population of 79,934 in 1900; two decades later it was at 159,842, most of it concentrated in Hidalgo, Willacy, Nueces, and Cameron counties. In this process of economic development, people of Mexican descent lost their property and accustomed livelihood as well as their political protection.[32]

These new arrivals called themselves "Progressives" and soon successfully challenged the old political ways of managing business in the Valley. Politics had long been practiced Texas-boss-style, which meant violating the state electoral laws at will, paying the poll taxes for Mexican-American supporters, recruiting illegal aliens to vote, tampering with results when all else failed, hiring gunmen to intimidate voters, and eliminating the opposition and embezzling from local treasuries to support the entire enterprise. James Wells was the prototype of just such a boss.[33]

Wells explains just how the masses of Mexican Americans fit into the scheme and reveals the mentality which reinforced it:

> I suppose they [the King Ranch people] control 500 votes, and they [the Mexicans who work there or live in the district] go to their major domos [sic], and they go to Mr. Caesar Kleberg, and to Robert Kleberg [King Ranch managers], and to Captain King—while he was living—and ask him whom they should vote for. The truth is, and very few people who don't live in that country know it, that it is the property owners and the intelligent people who in that way really do vote Mexicans . . . . The King people always protected their servants and helped them when they were sick and never let them go hungry, and they [the peons] always feel grateful, and they naturally don't need any buying, or selling or any coercion—they went to those that helped them when they needed help. . . . The Mexican naturally inherited from his ancestors from Spanish rule, the idea of looking to the head of the ranch—the place where he lived and got his living—for guidance and direction.[34]

And as for Boss Wells himself: "So far as being boss, if I exercise any influence among those people [Mexican-American voters] it's because in the 41 years I have lived among them I have tried to so conduct myself as to show them that I was their friend and they could trust me, I take no advantage of them or their ignorance. I buried many of them. It wasn't [only] two or three days before the election [that Wells extended such beneficence], but through the years around, and they have always been true to me . . . ."[35]

The newly arrived Progressives designed strategies to sever bosses like Wells from their Mexican-American political support. So while the region changed from ranching to farming, traditional politics were also rearranged. And the Mexican Revolution and the Plan of San Diego became embedded in all this ferment. According to the sociologist David Montejano, the resulting turmoil unleashed racist passions which had been controlled by social structures for two generations: "In the midst of a ranch society based on paternalistic work arrangements, there emerged a farm society based on contract labor and business rationality."[36] Displaced and angered Mexican-Americans responded with violence.

Montejano is provocative, but is he right? More disciplined archival research is required to find out. As yet the ethnicity of the raiders is unclear, as is their nationality. Relatively little is known of their socioeconomic status and even less of their motivation. Conditions in the Valley undoubtedly stirred Mexican-American resentment, but how that mixed with Anglo opportunism, Constitutionalist strategy, anarchist radicalism, or even German intrigue has yet to be measured.

When it came to violence during the epoch, the region's most acute shock came the night of October 18, 1915. Raiders, presumably Mexican, derailed a St. Louis, Brownsville and Mexico Railway train at Tandy's Crossing near a trestle bridge three miles north of Olmito. J. L. Allhands remembers that the raiders "removed the angle bars and spikes from a rail on the west side [of the tracks]. A wire was fastened to it [the rail] and then stretched to their ambuscade in the brush. A shovel was attached to the other end of the wire, in order that three or four of the bandits might get a firm hold and make a good job of pulling the rail when the ill-fated train arrived. Just as the on-rushing train rolled up they jerked this rail from under the moving engine. Upon hitting the ties, it was ditched and thrown at right angles to the main line. The baggage and mail cars were also toppled over on their sides."[37]

John I. Kleiber, a local district attorney, was riding in the smoker, located in the back half (blacks occupied the front half) of one of the train's two passenger cars, when the engine ran off the track. "I noticed that the train began to bump and slow up. I felt it slacken speed and began to bump quite violently, and listed—to use the nautical term—to my side . . . . At that moment the train stopped. Scattering shots and then irregular volleys broke out and increased in volume . . . . Four unmasked desperadoes entered the coaches, amid curses, yells and screams, and as if death had turned gunmen to finish the job, began shooting at the ducking passengers."[38]

Dr. Edgar S. McCain, the state quarantine officer at Brownsville; H. J. Wallace, a former Texas Ranger; and a teenage boy sought the refuge of a toilet at one end of the smoker. Kleiber continues: "They [the raiders] came to the [toilet] door and battered on [it]. Either the Mexican boy or Wallace opened the door, and as they did so, they [the bandits] dragged the Mexican boy out. He told them that he was a Mexican and that there were two *gringos* in there. I will say *gringos* is a term for Americans that the Mexican uses in contempt just as many Americans do 'greasers'—they immediately fired into the toilet. As I understand it, Wallace was standing on the lavatory, and he was shot in the shoulder. The shot that struck Dr. McCain [in the abdomen] went through the door [and mortally wounded him]."[39]

The robbers especially had it in for American soldiers and *gringo* passengers riding the train: "Maten los soldados, Americanos cabrones [Kill the soldiers, those American bastards]." However, when it came to loot, they did not discriminate among foreigners, excluding Mexicans. As for the Mexicans: "Mexicanos no [harm], gringos no más [mercy]."[40] Then the bandits, some fifty of them in all, made their getaway on horses and foot. They had killed three Americans and wounded four others. Passengers lost their jewelry, cash, and suitcases. All in all, it was the boldest raid yet by Mexicans into U.S. territory. Its connection to the Plan de San Diego is not clear. Nor is enough known about the social origins of the attackers. Mexicans from across the river? Texas-Mexicans from the region? Maybe some Anglos? American outsiders? Those bent on avenging the incident did not worry about such distinctions.

Retribution was quick and certain. Texas newspapers demanded eradication of the "mangy wolves," the "lice in the thickets," the "hounds of perdition"—all of which referred to individuals of Mexican ancestry in the Lower Rio Grande. A deputy sheriff announced that he would "get" nineteen Mexicans for every American shot in the raid. It was later reported that in one field he and his group killed eleven Mexican farmhands who seem to have had no possible connection to the derailment.[41] Posses swept through the countryside around the site of the train wreck, administering revenge as they went. Six suspected raiders were shot down in the pursuit; Texas Rangers captured four others and hanged them from trees as exemplary punishment. Sheriff W. T. Vann later testified before a state investigating committee that he had seen the executions but refused to take part. When he declined, a Ranger remarked, "If you do not have the guts to do it, I will."[42]

Meanwhile, residents of nearby Brownsville cowered in terror that they might be the next target of a full-scale Mexican onslaught. There was a report out of Matamoros that recruiters there offered a bonus of ten dollars in gold, plus 75 cents a day, and a division of spoils for those who would join the Army of Revolution in Texas.[43] Albert Brown, the city's mayor, called a meeting of local notables to plan a defense, and they hurried a plea for additional troops to Washington, D.C., which quickly responded with reinforcements. Before they could arrive, however, raiders had ambushed a U.S. Army cavalry patrol at Ojo de Agua, near Mission, killing three soldiers and wounding eight others. That carnage brought the military to further readiness. Army artillerymen sighted their cannons on Matamoros and the International Bridge, determined to repulse any invasion from the Mexican side.[44]

At the same time, the federal government also approached the border raids through diplomatic channels. Authorities must have recognized all along that the Plan of San Diego could not have functioned without a Mexican connection, and it was obvious that the Constitutionalists—the troops of Venustiano Carranza—controlled the territory in which the raiders sought refuge. Moreover, Mexican newspapers that supported Carranza propagandized in favor of the race war in Texas and reported its progress toward triumph. Then General Funston told superiors that he had information that the Constitutionalist commander in Matamoros, Emiliano P. Nafarrate, had himself directed some of the raids, even if he had not personally crossed the river. In fact, Nafarrate may have been linked to the plan since its inception. Finally came the train wreck; during the fracas the attackers any number of times had shouted "Viva Carranza!"[45]

Washington protested to the Constitutionalist chief, who in response transferred Nafarrate much farther south to Tampico. Moreover, Carranza let it be known through his special agents dealing with the U.S. government that, if it granted official diplomatic recognition, the raids might cease altogether. Precisely how the Wilson administration fit all the pieces together is not known, but on October 19 it accorded Carranza's movement de facto official diplomatic recognition, which meant that the United States now endorsed and would openly support Constitutionalist rule in Mexico. The Americans had apparently been inclined in that direction for some time, but Carranza used the Plan of San Diego to nudge them firmly into his camp.[46]

Proof of this tactic came later in 1916 after Pancho Villa had attacked the New Mexican border town of Columbus. The famous (or infamous, depending on your point of view) Pershing Expedition followed, and Carranza ordered the Americans out of his country. When the United States refused to budge, Carranza brandished a proven old weapon: the Plan of San Diego. Two Mexican Americans who had been associated with the former plan, Luis de la Rosa, a former Cameron County deputy sheriff, and Aniceto Pizaña, from a respected Brownsville-area ranching family, now worked for the *Carrancistas* to recruit forces for an invasion of Texas in the name of the plan. Preparations for such a maneuver proceeded apace until suddenly shelved by the *Carrancista* leadership, which did not really want outright war with the United States. Instead the Constitutionalists settled for regenerating the border raids. In mid-June, 1916, marauders struck, first around Brownsville and then south of Laredo. They soon learned, however, that U.S. response tactics had changed; instead of only driving the raiders back into Mexico, they now followed in "hot pursuit" right across the Rio Grande. Now war between the United States and Mexico truly threatened.

The U.S. Army War College drew up a plan for the invasion of Mexico, and Woodrow Wilson federalized the nation's state guards and ordered them to the border. More than 100,000 militiamen soon arrived, the largest mobilization of American might up to that time. Brownsville's Fort Brown had been reactivated. A diplomatic flurry followed, and by July the Constitutionalists had decided not to press the Plan of San Diego any further. Once again, it had served its immediate purpose; it had, among other factors, forced the U.S. government to deal with the *Carrancistas* at the highest levels.[47]

Or at least this is what some good scholars who have analyzed the plan tend to think. They emphasize the role of Carranza. Others are not so positive; at least they would pay more attention to Germany's attempts to distract the U.S. military from war in Europe by causing unrest along the border, or U.S. labor unrest stimulated by the International Workers of the World, the Mexican supporters of the radical Ricardo Flores Magón, and their likes, or even Japanese meddling in hemispheric affairs. Still others spot machinations of the followers of the deposed Victoriano Huerta in the plan, while the irredentism of Mexican and Mexican Americans is also being weighed in. Certainly the sentiments of a severely disrupted Mexican-American population in the valley need to be considered. Finally, there were the opportunists. Early on Secretary of State Lansing suspected as much when he noted that "lawless people" were using the troubles in the valley to plunder and steal, "and we are not sure that all the law breakers are Mexicans. Some of them, we know, are not."[48]

Whatever the origins of the plan itself, it contributed to the frightful human price being paid for "troubles" in the region. Cecilia Rendón and her family counted among the thousands of Mexican Americans uprooted by the turmoil in the Valley. She recounts, "Many families abandoned their farms and lost their belongings. We had lots of cows, chickens, and pigs. Everything was left behind."[49] Under the pressures of those times, perhaps 7,000 or more left their homesteads and livelihoods, their ranchos and *trabajo,* for good. Some settled in the towns and cities of the region, but most returned to uncertain and insecure lives in Mexico, where the government offered them stopgap services and land for subsistence. The property and opportunities they were forced to abandon soon fell into the hands of enterprising Anglos, some of whom seem all along to have savored the region's increasing land values based in agricultural potential.

The sordid story concerning these happenings has never been told in all of its particulars. In fact, we would know much less about it if shortly thereafter the Texas Rangers had not received their comeuppance. These Rangers had always been the front line of defense for the relatively few Anglos who dominated the citizens of Mexican descent who comprised the great bulk of the Valley's population. But when in 1918, Texas governor William Hobby for his own political purposes employed the Rangers to discourage Mexican voting in the Valley, the local elites turned against their former benefactors. As one example, the same J. T. Canales, the Brownsville attorney who had earlier raised his own troops to assist the Rangers in combating the border raiders, lamented, "The Rangers have adopted a policy that is a shame and disgrace to my native state and to my American citizenship."[50] Then in testimony given to a state legislative committee, he and others laid bare the inhumane deeds of the constabulary. The legislative committee concluded: "From its inception, the policies of the Ranger force have been the same, and these are now accepted as traditional, 'Get your man and keep no records except of final results.'"[51] The hearings led to a radical reformation of the organization in 1919.

The people of the Lower Rio Grande who emerged in control of the Valley's affairs tended rather quickly to put aside these unhappy events and instead began to focus upon the undeniable progress and development which has marked the region. But Robert Runyon had already engraved images of those troubled times on film, where they are still preserved and can be addressed and pondered.

In the fall of 1915 widespread raiding erupted in the Lower Rio Grande Valley. Its causes are still being debated; some rebels adhered to a so-called Plan of San Diego (named for the South Texas town), whose supporters meant to carve a new republic from territory lost by Mexico to the U.S. in the 1848 war between the two countries. It was to be a country populated by American minority groups: Mexican Americans, blacks, and Indians. White males over sixteen years old would be killed. Revenge for alleged oppression was the motive. Other observers claim the unrest was caused by the Mexican Constitutionalists who aimed to force official U.S.diplomatic recognition of their cause; still others believe that German complicity was intended to keep the U.S. busy along the border and away from Europe's world war. Whatever the cause, the results were for many Valley residents catastrophic, and Robert Runyon recorded the history of these unsavory events with his camera, here the attack on August 8, 1915, of a railway flag station called Las Norias along the St. Louis, Brownsville and Mexico Railway line, about seventy miles north of Brownsville. At Las Norias perhaps sixty raiders attacked a picket of eight army soldiers and a few local law enforcement officials, seriously wounding several before being driven off by reinforcements who reached the post in the nick of time to prevent its destruction.

Six of the army cavalrymen who survived the Las Norias attack later posed for Runyon on the steps to the station house. The raiders had not expected to encounter any military presence at the flag station, and when they did, they suffered considerable casualties, and reportedly lost between five and ten men. Las Norias marked the northernmost advance of the insurgents into the United States and placed them well within the boundaries of the famous Kenedy-King Ranch, the single strongest symbol of Anglo power in the region. Courtesy of the Barker Texas History Center.

Local officials deputized individuals and individuals deputized themselves to join the struggle against the raiders in the Valley. Law enforcement became a crazy-quilt activity with units often more in competition than in coordination with one another. Here an unidentified volunteer poses at the ready-wait outside the ranch house at Las Norias. Courtesy of the Barker Texas History Center.

In one of their boldest attacks of the epoch, the raiders derailed a St. Louis, Brownsville and Mexico train just six miles north of Brownsville on October 18, 1915. Then some twenty raiders boarded the train and rounded up and robbed the passengers. During the tumult, shots were fired, and as a result a Brownsville doctor and an army soldier died; other militiamen and civilians lay seriously injured. Now all Brownsville literally cowered in fear of a full-scale invasion from the Mexican side. Courtesy of the Barker Texas History Center.

VIEW OF THE WRECK BY
MEXICAN BADITS

Just how the raiders worked their derailment can be seen in this picture. They literally yanked one rail out from under the locomotive. First they removed the spikes that held the rail in place. Then they looped a strong wire around the loose end of the rail and stretched the wire to a shovel dug in behind a large rock. As the train approached at thirty-five miles an hour, they pulled on the shovel to turn the rail outward. As a result, the engine derailed along with two other cars. On former occasions the raiders had burned railroad bridges to upset communications, but in this case they managed to derail and loot a specific train. The *Houston Post* featured Runyon's photos on page one of its October 23 edition. Courtesy of the Barker Texas History Center.

Reprisals for the raids were not long in coming. The Army mobilized National Guard units and beefed up patrols on the border. State and local units joined the effort. So did the famed Texas Rangers, who shot first and asked questions later. The Rangers, derisively called "Rinches" by their victims, rode roughshod over the modest dirt farmers in the Valley, who were mainly of Mexican origin. The Rangers imposed their own brand of lynch law on suspects and innocent alike—and were proud to do so—as can be seen in this famous Runyon photo which circulated the nation as a picture postcard. At the left rides Texas Ranger captain J. M. Fox, who once telephoned this daily report: "We got another Mexican, but he's dead." Courtesy of the Barker Texas History Center.

Anticipating an all-out attack by Mexicans on Brownsville, this army artillery unit sighted on the international bridge across the Rio Grande and targets in Matamoros, ready to start the shelling when given the word. Official U.S. recognition of the Constitutionalists eased the tension, and the invasion threat waned but never disappeared. The troops continued their training exercises just in case—and also because World War I invited U.S. intervention. Courtesy of the Barker Texas History Center.

It will never be known to how many "suspects" the Rangers and their compatriots delivered their brand of summary justice. Following the spectacular train wreck outside of Brownsville, the Rangers captured seven men who they claimed had participated in the raid. The next day four of the captives were discovered dead, their bodies riddled with bullets. Estimates are that the Rangers handled more than three hundred individuals in the same manner. Courtesy of the Barker Texas History Center.

Locals mixed with Texas Rangers to reestablish domestic order and to take reprisals in the Valley. In doing so they caused thousands of rural people to leave their property and to take refuge in Brownsville or on the Mexican side of the line. Many never returned to their holdings. Land they vacated later became the property of large-scale agricultural entrepreneurs. Courtesy of the Hidalgo County Historical Museum.

Mexicans and Americans kept a close eye on one another from their respective sides of the Rio Grande. From time to time they cussed each other out and threatened to cross the river to make their insults stick. Mexican soldiers claimed they had no quarrel with the U.S. military but vowed revenge against the Texas Rangers and members of the local citizenry. Courtesy of the Hidalgo County Historical Museum.

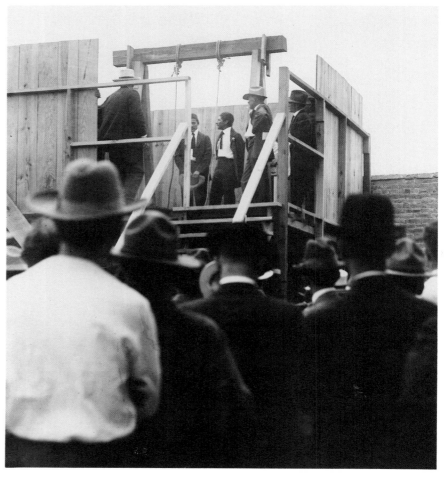

The state also weighed in with its form of justice. On August 6, 1915, a band of fourteen raiders robbed the general store at Sebastian and then took two of the local Anglos prisoner, A. L. Austin and his son, Charlie. A short time later the robbers murdered the Austins. Citizens howled for revenge, but it took almost a year to exact it. The victims were two Mexicans, José Buenrostro and Melquiades Chapa, arrested for alleged banditry. But "eye witnesses" suddenly implicated them in the Austin killings. As a result, Buenrostro and Chapa were tried and convicted of murder and publicly hanged on May 19, 1916, in the yard of the new Brownsville jail. Hundreds turned out for the execution, and Runyon caught the moment with his camera. Courtesy of the Barker Texas History Center.

While dressed for their hanging, José Buenrostro and Melquiades Chapa posed for Runyon in a small chapel provided for their last prayers. Note that Runyon blocked out the glaring light from a main window to get a better image of the condemned pair. Courtesy of the Barker Texas History Center.

The U.S. War Department dispatched regulars and then militiamen in force to the border area in 1915 and 1916. Here they are seen marching on East Elizabeth Street in downtown Brownsville on their way to the Fort Brown encampment which bordered town. On more than one occasion during their stay there, federal commanders found themselves in conflict with state and local authorities who advocated a more aggressive policy (meaning an invasion) toward Mexico. The street scene recorded by Runyon reveals much of the ambiance of the times, and the city still retains much of its lovely architectural diversity along with its share of cantinas. Courtesy of the Brownsville Historical Association.

The raiders took considerable toll among the military, killing several dozen soldiers along the Rio Grande. Private Arthur Kraft was sleeping in a shed deep in a cotton field on Galveston Ranch when thirty raiders struck his ten-man patrol. In the initial exchange of fire, a bullet caught Kraft in the head. Seriously wounded, he whispered to a buddy: "I'm shot. Stick by me and I'll stick by you." After a half-hour skirmish, the soldiers drove off their assailants, but Kraft, who had been in the army only four months, died and was given these full military honors photographed by Runyon. Courtesy of the Barker Texas History Center.

CROWDS GEATHERED AT DEPOT TO SEE PRIV. STUBBLEFIELDS LEAVE FOR BIG STONE GAP. VA.

While on patrol in Hidalgo County, Lieutenant W. King of the Twenty-Sixth Infantry returned to the Saenz store at Progreso and found Private Henry Stubblefield of Big Stone Gap, Virginia, dead and another soldier wounded, victims of raiders who still roamed the area. Suddenly, all hell broke loose. Some seventy-five Mexicans opened fire on the U.S. contingent of only nine soldiers, wounding several before retreating to their side of the Rio Grande. In the aftermath the Americans discovered that one of their encampments on the river had been overrun and one soldier taken prisoner. The Mexicans reportedly mutilated the militaryman's body and displayed his head on a pike like a trophy across the river. Meanwhile, Runyon photographed Private Stubblefield's funeral cortege. Courtesy of the Barker Texas History Center.

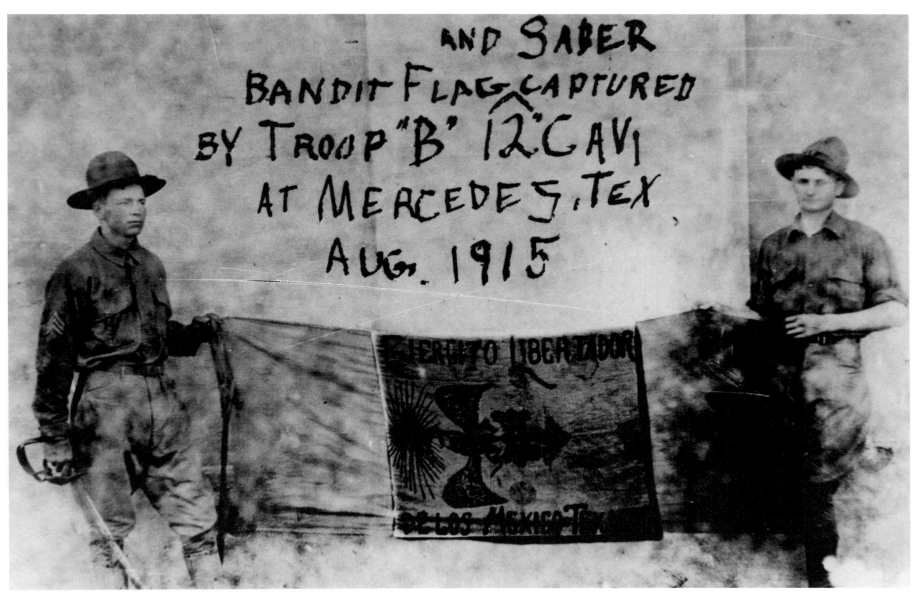

BANDIT FLAG CAPTURED
BY TROOP "B" 12 CAV
AT MERCEDES, TEX
AUG. 1915

EJERCITO LIBERTADOR
DE LOS MEXICO TEX

With the capture of this battle flag, army cavalrymen proved that the raiders, at least some of them, aimed for revolutionary social reform. "Land and Liberty" was the battle cry of the anarchists who were at that time active in various sectors of the United States and Mexico, not to speak of other parts of the world. Those in the Valley may well have been influenced by the nucleus headed by Ricardo Flores Magón, who had been exiled from Mexico by the Porfirian dictatorship and later established headquarters in Los Angeles. Courtesy of the Hidalgo County Historical Museum.

Hostilities lessened in late October 1915 after the United States had granted diplomatic recognition to Venustiano Carranza, leading some to believe that all along he had been behind the depredations. In a display of sudden but certainly tenuous friendship, Carranza (with beard) met with Colonel A. P. Blockston (left of Carranza), who commanded Fort Brown, on the International Bridge between Brownsville and Matamoros on November 30, 1915. The man at Carranza's right shoulder is General Emiliano A. P. Nafarrate, who commanded the Constitutionalist garrison at Brownsville and is said to have orchestrated the raids. Peering out in eyeglasses (fifth from right) is Jess Johnson, the U.S. consul at Matamoros. Courtesy of the Barker Texas History Center.

One result of the turmoil was that thousands of Mexicans and Mexican Americans under harassment and worse by the Texas Rangers and others fled their property and livelihood in the Valley for the safety of Mexico. It is estimated that 7,000 people like these crossed the International Bridge in search of sanctuary. Some undoubtedly later returned, but as few of them held legal titles to their land or possessed the funds necessary to defend their holdings in court, they lost everything to Anglo entrepreneurs anxious to develop the rich, well-irrigated land, now tied to a broadening national communications network. Courtesy of the Barker Texas History Center.

3. Rebellion and Retaliation

1. For a general overview see Stambaugh and Stambaugh, *The Lower Rio Grande Valley of Texas*. Two better accounts by contemporary observers are W. H. Chatfield, ed., *Twin Cities of the Border—Brownsville, Texas, and Matamoros, Mexico—and the Country of the Lower Rio Grande;* and Pierce, *A Brief History of the Lower Rio Grande Valley.* For a handsome photographic account, see Robertson, *Rio Grande Heritage.* An excellent broad, sociological perspective is offered by David Montejano, *Anglos and Mexicans in the Making of Texas.*

2. The best overviews of these events are Linda B. Hall and Don M. Coerver, *Revolution on the Border: The United States and Mexico, 1910–1920;* and Coerver and Hall, *Texas and the Mexican Revolution.*

3. Charles H. Harris III and Louis R. Sadler, "The Plan of San Diego and the Mexican–United States War Crisis of 1916: A Reexamination," in *The Border and the Revolution,* p. 71.

4. J. J. Sanders, Capt., Co. A, R. F., to Henry Hutchings, Mar. 1, 1913, Texas Ranger Correspondence, 1913–1917, Adjutant General's Office, Webb (Walter Prescott) Papers, File 2R290, BTHC.

5. Besides Harris and Sadler, "The Plan of San Diego," pp. 71–98, major works on the Plan of San Diego include Douglas W. Richmond, *"La guerra de Texas se renova;* Mexican Insurrection and Carrancista Ambitions, 1900–1920," *Aztlán* 11 (Spring 1980): 1–32; Rodolfo Rocha, "Banditry in the Lower Rio Grande Valley of Texas, 1915," *Studies in History* 6 (1976): 55–73; James A. Sandos, "The Plan de San Diego: War and Diplomacy on the Texas Border, 1915–1916," *Arizona and the West* 14 (Spring 1972): 5–24; Juan Gómez Quiñones, "The Plan of San Diego Renewed," *Aztlán* 1 (Spring 1970): 124–132; Allen Gerlach, "Conditions along the Border—1915: The Plan of San Diego," *New Mexico Historical Review* 43 (July 1968): 195–212; William A. Hager, "The Plan of San Diego: Unrest on the Texas Border in 1915," *Arizona and the West* 5 (Winter 1963): 327–336; Charles C. Cumberland, "Border Raids in the Lower Rio Grande Valley—1915," *Southwestern Historical Quarterly* 57 (Jan. 1954): 301–324.

An interesting critique of several of these articles is offered by Jake Watts, "The Plan of San Diego and the Lower Rio Grande Valley," in *More Studies in Brownsville History,* ed. Milo Kearney, pp. 322–345. Watts translates the plan into English in his article.

Two fine doctoral dissertations as well as Montejano's monograph also consider the plan in their treatment of broader issues. See James A. Sandos, "The Mexican Revolution and the United States, 1915–1917: The Impact of Conflict in the Tamaulipas-Texas Frontier upon the Emergence of Revolutionary Governments in Mexico"; and Rocha, "The Influence of the Mexican Revolution."

6. *Brownsville Herald,* July 1, 1915.

7. Ibid., July 9, 1915.

8. Sandos develops the concept in "The Mexican Revolution and the United States." For a refinement see Montejano, *Anglos and Mexicans,* p. 176.

9. *Brownsville Herald,* July 29, 1915.

10. See note 5 for this chapter. All of these works detail the incidents referred to in this chapter and more. For observations of a contemporary observer see Pierce, *A Brief History,* esp. chaps. 10, 11.

11. *Brownsville Herald,* July 24, 1915.

12. Ibid., Aug. 7, 1915.

13. Ibid., Aug. 3, 1915.

14. See note 5 for this chapter.

15. Allhands, *Gringo Builders,* pp. 265–266.

16. Ibid., p. 266.

17. Quoted in Sandos, "The Mexican Revolution and the United States," p. 164.

18. *Brownsville Herald,* Oct. 2, 1915.

19. *Houston Post,* Sept. 4, 1915.

20. *Brownsville Herald,* Sept. 27, 1915, Sept. 29, 1915, Oct. 1, 1915.

21. Hall and Coerver, *Revolution on the Border,* p. 24; *Houston Post,* Sept. 8, 1915.

22. *Brownsville Herald,* Oct. 2, 1915; quoted in Rocha, "Banditry," p. 67.

23. Quoted in Oscar J. Martínez, *Fragments of the Mexican Revolution: Personal Accounts from the Border,* pp. 171–172.

24. Ibid., p. 172.

25. Ibid.

26. Quoted in Montejano, *Anglos and Mexicans,* p. 102.

27. Ibid. For hurling of curses across the river, see *Brownsville Herald,* Aug. 14, 1915.

28. *Brownsville Herald,* Sept. 16, 1915.

29. Walter Prescott Webb, *The Texas Rangers: A Century of Frontier Defense,* p. 478.

30. Harris and Sadler, "The Plan of San Diego," p. 82.

31. Ibid.

32. Montejano, *Anglos and Mexicans,* pp. 101–155.

33. Evan Anders, "Boss Rule and Constituent Interests: South Texas Politics during the Progressive Era," *Southwestern Historical Quarterly* 74 (Jan. 1981): 269–292; Montejano, *Anglos and Mexicans,* pp. 129–155.

34. Quoted in Anders, "Boss Rule," pp. 274–275.

35. Ibid., p. 284.

36. Ibid., p. 109.

37. Allhands, *Gringo Builders,* pp. 266–267. The train wreck is reported in the *Brownsville Herald,* Aug. 19 and 20, 1915.

38. *Brownsville Herald,* Oct. 20, 1915; and quoted in Martínez, *Fragments of the Mexican Revolution,* p. 154.

39. Quoted in Martínez, *Fragments of the Mexican Revolution,* p. 156.

40. Ibid.

41. Rocha, "Banditry," p. 68.

42. Stambaugh and Stambaugh, *The Lower Rio Grande Valley,* p. 229; and John Busby McClung, "The Rangers along the Rio Grande, 1910–1919," p. 84.

43. *Brownsville Herald,* Oct. 19, 1915.

44. *Houston Post,* Sept. 21, 1915.

45. A. S. Garza to Basilio Ramos, Jan. 15, 1915, Texas Ranger Correspondence, 1913–1917, Adjutant General's Office, Webb (Walter Prescott) Papers, File 2R290, BTHC.

46. Harris and Sadler, "The Plan of San Diego," pp. 76–80; Martínez, *Fragments of the Mexican Revolution,* p. 154.

47. Harris and Sadler, "The Plan of San Diego," pp. 82–98; Coerver and Hall, *Texas and the Mexican Revolution,* pp. 101–106.

48. *Brownsville Herald,* Aug. 11, 1915.

49. Quoted in Martínez, *Fragments of the Mexican Revolution,* p. 172.

50. Quoted in ibid., p. 164.

51. Julian Samora, Joe Bernal, and Albert Peña, *Gunpowder Justice: A Reassessment of the Texas Rangers,* p. 77. Proceedings of the investigation have not been published. For the manuscript of the report, see "Proceedings of the Joint Committee of the Senate and House in the Investigation of the Texas State Ranger Force, 1919," Texas State Archives, Austin.

4. Military Buildup in the Lower Rio Grande Valley

The large military buildup in the Lower Rio Grande Valley that made possible the boom in Robert Runyon's postcard sales in the summer and fall of 1916 did not result from the earlier violence and loss of life in the Lower Rio Grande Valley. Those "troubles" did produce a modest influx of troops to the Brownsville area and a corresponding increase in customers for Runyon's cards, but both were on a small scale compared with what occurred in mid-1916.

Nearly five years before, in October 1911, President William Howard Taft, acting on the advice of the War Department, had signed an executive order declaring Fort Brown "useless for military purposes" and transferring it to the jurisdiction of the Department of the Interior.[1] When an apparent threat to the lives and property of American residents of Matamoros in February 1913 led to the dispatch of a 175-man cavalry troop to reactivate Fort Brown, the U.S. Army had only 4,000 soldiers available to patrol the entire border from Texas to California. The small number of military personnel assigned to defend the international boundary as of that date was a legacy of the good diplomatic relations that existed between the United States and Mexico and the generally tranquil conditions that prevailed along the border during most of the Porfiriato. By 1914, however, General Díaz had been in exile for three years, and the Mexican Revolution had begun to spill over the frontier to American territory, especially in the Brownsville area. In late April General Tasker Bliss, commander of the Southern Department of the Army, sent seven hundred troops from his headquarters at Fort Sam Houston in San Antonio to beef up the small garrison at Fort Brown. He acted as a result of what proved to be false rumors circulating along the border that the recent U.S. invasion and continuing occupation of Veracruz would lead to retaliatory raids across the Rio Grande by Mexican forces or major disturbances by Mexican residents of the Lower Valley. The violence associated with the revolution that plagued the region around Brownsville in 1915 and early 1916 produced a further increase of U.S. Army troop strength at Fort Brown to 1,900 officers and men by the beginning of May 1916. This still relatively modest force was charged with maintaining security throughout the area and patrolling a 110-mile stretch of the border from southeast of Brownsville to Rio Grande City.[2]

The large influx of troops to the Lower Rio Grande Valley in the summer of 1916 was a part of the massive military buildup along the entire southern border of the United States. On March 9, 1916, forces acting under the orders of Pancho Villa attacked Columbus, New Mexico, and killed seventeen American soldiers and civilians. By March 15, the first elements of a contingent of more than 12,000 Army regulars under General John J. Pershing had crossed the border with orders to mount a "punitive expedition" into Mexico. Then on May 5, *villistas* raided Glenn Springs and Boquillas in the Big Bend country of Texas. Two days later President Woodrow Wilson ordered a partial mobilization of the National Guard; a total of 5,260 men from units in Texas, Arizona, and New Mexico rallied to the colors. After assessing the situation, Wilson decided that these guardsmen and all available regular Army troops were insufficient in number to protect the 3,000-mile-long border from attack from forces loyal to Villa or Venustiano Carranza, his rival for leadership of the revolution in Mexico. On June 18, he ordered the mobilization of the National Guards of the remaining states to implement his policy of "watchful waiting." By late August nearly 16,000 regulars and 184,000 guardsmen were on duty in camps from Texas to California. Although the War Department assigned some of these troops to small, strategically positioned outposts, it concentrated the great majority of them in four locations: the vicinities of Douglas, Arizona, and El Paso, San Antonio, and Brownsville, Texas.[3]

On May 20, Brigadier General James S. ("Gallopin' Jim") Parker assumed command of the newly created Brownsville District with headquarters at Fort Brown. By August he had responsibility for a force of 28,000 National Guard troops and Army regulars assigned to the fort itself and to several smaller camps at Rio Grande City, Harlingen, Mission, Mercedes, McAllen, Donna, Pharr, San Benito, and on the outskirts of Brownsville. Two thousand of Parker's men were Army regulars while the rest were guardsmen from Texas, Iowa, Illinois, Virginia, Oklahoma, North Dakota, South Dakota, Louisiana, Nebraska, Minnesota, and Indiana. General Parker shared responsibility for the defense of the Lower Rio Grande Valley with Major General John F. O'Ryan, commander of the 12,000-man-strong New York National Guard Division, which had individual units stationed at Mercedes, McAllen, Mission, Pharr, Hidalgo, Progreso, and Llano Grande.[4]

Many of the guardsmen assigned to the Lower Valley and other points on the border arrived hoping to get into a quick fight with the Mexicans and return home covered with glory. But contrary to their hopes, none of them ever entered combat. The invasion of U.S. territory that they expected to defend against never occurred; nor did any War Department order permit them to advance southward into Mexico. Instead they camped on the northern side of the international line fighting nothing but the heat, the rain, the mud, and the numerous animal pests. The men drilled, dug trenches, and became increasingly bored and disgruntled. Guardsmen in the Brownsville area, whose frequent periods of idleness gave them ample opportunity to pose for Robert Runyon's informal postcard portraits of themselves and their buddies, soon began to feel that they were wasting their time. Officers and men who had willingly and patriotically come to the border, often at real personal sacrifice, soon were anxious to return to their loved ones and normal occupations. Letters from home brought news of family troubles and particularly of financial problems, as employers failed to live up to promises with respect to paying salaries and holding open jobs.[5]

By early August General Parker decided that he could no longer ignore the widespread expressions of discontent among the troops and the recurrent rumors originating in the camps that certain units would soon be sent home. In an effort to bolster sagging morale, he issued a brief statement attributed to certain senior officers at the War Department in Washington which asserted that the deployment of the National Guard on the border was based on military necessity and that its duration could not be forecast. The men were put on notice that no plan existed to permit any of them to return home in the near future.[6]

Instead of strengthening morale, this tactless expression of official policy apparently led to its further erosion, and ten days later General Parker felt obliged to explain directly to his troops why they were on the border. He acknowledged that some of the men under his command believed that their failure to go into combat proved that they served no useful purpose in the Lower Rio Grande Valley. He dismissed this point of view with the assertion that his troops' presence in the area and willingness to fight were well known to the enemies of the United States and had deterred them from attacks on American lives and property. As long as these unnamed enemies continued to be active, his troops would have to remain where they were. General Parker also noted that a few of the younger enlisted men under his command suffered from homesickness. He sternly admonished them to grow up and behave like men.[7]

The statement of the commanding officer of the Brownsville District did nothing to improve morale, even temporarily, and as time passed, growing numbers of guardsmen appear to have become increasingly dissatisfied with the circumstances of their duty on the border. That was certainly the reaction of men in two units, the First

Illinois Cavalry and the Seventh New York Infantry, for whose service in the Lower Rio Grande Valley reliable documentation exists.

The First Illinois Cavalry came to the border with the reputation as one of the finer regiments in the entire National Guard. Many of the officers and noncommissioned officers were veterans of the regular army; some had combat experience in the Spanish American War. They mobilized in Springfield on June 27, entrained there on July 1, and arrived in Brownsville on July 4, becoming one of the first Guard units to arrive in the Lower Valley. As they marched from the railroad station to their assigned campsite three miles north of town on the Alice road, they made an impressive and confident picture of robust American military men. Brownsville residents who saw them pass felt reassured by their presence and marveled at their modern equipment, especially the five machine guns purchased especially for the regiment by private subscription.[8]

The first indication that the conditions of their service on the border would not meet their expectations came when they confronted the bleakness of their campsite. Like most arriving guardsmen, the men of the First Illinois Cavalry had to construct or assemble virtually everything they needed for subsistence from the ground up. The suddenness and the scope of the military buildup meant that advance preparations for the arrival of the troops were usually extremely limited. In the case of the First Illinois Cavalry, that meant sleeping in hastily erected tents and making do with primitive latrine, bathing, and mess facilities.

Only two days after their arrival, while they were still struggling to adapt to their new environment, the guardsmen were assaulted by swarming gnats that got into their eyes and developed a particular fondness for taking baths in ink wells in the officers' tents. Colonel Milton J. Foreman, who commanded the First Illinois Cavalry, tried to put the best face on things when questioned by a local reporter. He said: "Any little annoyance we are experiencing from gnats is more than counterbalanced by the gratification of finding the camp absolutely free of mosquitos."[9] Nevertheless, several of the troops complained to the same reporter about the gnats and about having to be careful where they walked because of the danger of stepping

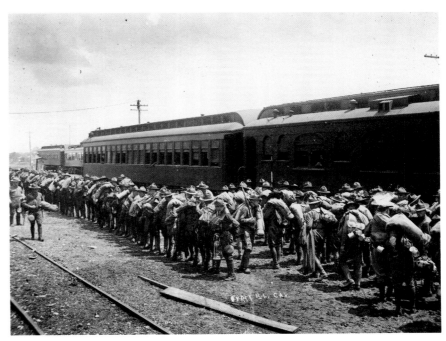

The arrival of the First Illinois Cavalry Regiment (dismounted) in Brownsville on July 4, 1916. This photograph shows the men as they are about to leave the railroad yard for their campsite north of town. Courtesy of the Barker Texas History Center.

on cactus plants, mesquite brush, and rattlesnakes. One soldier confided that two tarantulas had found their way past the sentries before being dispatched by an off-duty enlisted man.[10]

The discomforts of camp life might have been less irritating had the troops of the First Illinois Cavalry been able to carry out the military mission for which they had long trained. They had left home without their mounts, ostensibly to speed their journey to the border. When they got to Brownsville, General Parker, apparently in good faith, informed them that they would soon receive horses of a breed that was especially well suited to the hot climate of the Lower Valley. These animals were to be purchased from the stock of the Kenedy-King Ranch, 125 miles to the north.[11] Despite these assurances, the

DINNER TIME, FIRST ILL. CAV.

Many of the citizen-soldiers of the First Illinois Cavalry had to put up with conditions that they had never encountered back home. Among their major complaints was the chow. Courtesy of the Barker Texas History Center.

men of the First Illinois Cavalry discovered that the procurement of their mounts had been delayed. Major General Hugh L. Scott, the Army chief of staff, had a low opinion of the National Guard and even stated publicly that six months of training would be necessary to prepare any of its units for combat.[12] Consequently, it is not surprising that the allocation of funds to purchase horses for a cavalry regiment that had the misfortune to arrive on the border dismounted was not a high War Department priority, and the unit had to wait for more than five weeks before the promised delivery finally took place.

During that interval the First Illinois Cavalry became for all practical purposes an infantry regiment, much to the consternation of its officers and enlisted men, who, like other infantrymen in the Lower Valley, made practice marches in the summer heat and rain to such points as Palo Alto and Point Isabel. In the words of the official history of their unit, they "engaged in field exercises, target practice, combat firing maneuvers, and other activities incident to the highest type of intensive training."[13] Under the circumstances, discontent became rampant, and the belated arrival of the horses in August did little to improve matters. When the troops of the First Illinois Cavalry boarded a northbound train in Brownsville on October 17, 1916, they had one strong sentiment in common with departing guardsmen all along the border from Texas to California: they were bored and fed up with their duty and very anxious to return home.[14]

The experiences of the soldiers of the First Illinois Cavalry in the Lower Valley were in many respects similar to those of the men of the Seventh New York Infantry Regiment. Because of its large size and the presumed advanced state of its training, the New York National Guard came to the Lower Rio Grande Valley organized as a division with its own commanding officer. Major General John F. O'Ryan was not subordinate to General Parker, head of the Brownsville District, but instead had the privilege of reporting directly to General Frederick Funston, commander of the Southern Department of the Army.[15] The Seventh New York Infantry, a New York City regiment, enjoyed a reputation as a crack outfit.[16] Neverthe-

less, its previous military duties had been largely ceremonial. The 1,267 officers and men had plenty of experience drilling at their armory on Park Avenue, attending dances there on Saturday nights, and marching in the parades that took place on patriotic holidays. Nicknamed the "Grey Jackets," the unit was known throughout Manhattan for its smart dress uniforms.[17]

When a regiment made up of city-slickers—white-collar workers and professionals for the most part—arrived on July 2 at their campsite in McAllen, a small cattle town sixty miles up the river from Brownsville, many of the men felt that they had reached the end of the earth.[18] Corporal John B. Phillips, Jr., of Company B explained his reaction: "It is almost impossible to adequately describe the feeling of depression engendered by a glimpse of the flat, desolate-looking country of this part of Texas. A native said that it takes an Easterner three months to get over their depression, but we've heard many friends say it could not be done in a lifetime."[19]

Despite general unhappiness about their new surroundings, the New Yorkers soon settled down to their duties. Within a few weeks a city of tents where the officers and men slept, wooden houses for the commanding officer and his second-in-command, two Y.M.C.A. buildings, a guard house, a storage house for supplies, a post exchange, two moving-picture theaters, and several canteens had been constructed by the troops themselves with some help from a few skilled local civilians.[20]

Even before that task had been completed, the troops of the Seventh Infantry Regiment began a period of strenuous training, frequently in temperatures that reached 110 degrees Fahrenheit and occasionally in the knee-deep mud that resulted from torrential rains in the Lower Valley in the summer of 1916. As they drilled, paraded, and spent long hours on the firing range, the men grumbled. Most of all, they complained about the loneliness and boredom of guard duty at remote crossing points on the Rio Grande and the extreme discomfort and utter fatigue they had to endure during the bi-monthly ten-day training marches. In their free time the troops went to the Y.M.C.A., hung around the canteens with their buddies, watched moving pictures, cheered for their regiment's baseball team,

The arrival of the Seventh New York Infantry Regiment at McAllen on July 2, 1916. Some of the men talk or take their first good look at the desolate terrain while others, exhausted from the long train ride, try to sleep as they await orders from their officers to begin to set up camp. Courtesy of the Barker Texas History Center.

or just sat in their tents reading or writing postcards to friends and loved ones. Because of the distance from McAllen to Brownsville, excursions for the boys to that metropolis of the Lower Valley and to Matamoros were infrequent.[21] The routine of camp life on the border was hardly an exciting one for the New Yorkers and certainly not what they had anticipated when they left home.

Shortly after midnight on August 15, the nine members of the headquarters guard of the Seventh Infantry Regiment suddenly had some unexpected excitement. They actually thought for a few minutes that they were in combat with a band of Mexican invaders. Upon hearing shots from the direction of the border, the sergeant of the guard ordered the eight sentries under his command to follow him to the south side of the headquarters building. As they did so and more shots rang out, the men loaded and locked their weapons, formed a skirmish line, and awaited the attacking enemy. But no one appeared except a large number of sleepy guardsmen, who piled out of their tents in various stages of undress to find out what the commotion was all about. The next day an investigation revealed the cause of the mysterious gunfire. Several members of the First New York Field Artillery, who were camped nearby and had just been paid, shot their weapons in the air after an evening of heavy drinking. There were no enemy invaders after all.[22]

The members of the headquarters guard came as close as any members of the Seventh New York Infantry Regiment to combat with Mexicans. Moments of excitement, even of the type that occurred in the early morning hours of August 15, were rare, and as time went on the men became increasingly restless. As one of them put it, "Several efforts have been made to bury General Rumor, but he seems as elusive as Villa, and we fear the only hope of his demise

Not all the postcards that the guardsmen bought had pictures on them. Runyon had this one printed up to sell to the troops on his regular visits to the camps. The verse on the card, sung to the tune of "When You Wore a Tulip," accurately expressed the feelings of many of the guardsmen who came to the Brownsville area in the summer of 1916. Courtesy of the Barker Texas History Center.

For How Long the Lord Only Knows

AIR—"When you Wore a Tulip."

We left our homes and work back in old
    Iowa town,
Now the sun is burning down, for we're in
    Brownsville town;
The drilling and the hikings' putting humps
    upon our back,
We eat canned willie, beans and old hard
    tack.
Time has changed our willingness, we're
    not "too proud to fight,"
Just let us go to Mexico, we'll show them
    that we're right.

CHORUS,

Now you're in the army and I'm in the army,
We wear regulation clothes,
When they inspect us they have to respect us,
For our duties we all know,
We clean our rifles and do other trifles,
Its down where the cactus grows,
And there's no getting around it, we all have to
    stand it.—
For how long the Lord only knows.

The rainy season's here now and it sure
    has caused a flood,
The fever's in our blood, we're living in the
    mud.
The lizards, snakes and scorpions, they
    surely are a fright,
Mosquitos sing our lullaby each night,
Yet we are thankful for one thing, that
    none of us are ill,
For every cut or bruise or pain, they cure
    us with a pill!

is an order for us to entrain for New York, and while for a young man with few responsibilities this experience is of incalculable value, it's pretty fair to say that 99.99-100 per cent of the troops here would greet such an order with perfervid enthusiasm."[23]

The orders which the men of the Seventh New York Infantry as well as guardsmen all along the Mexican border eagerly awaited finally began to be issued. In the Lower Rio Grande Valley the first soldiers allowed to break camp and return home, members of Guard regiments from Texas, Louisiana, and New York, departed in late August.[24] The Seventh New York Infantry left McAllen on November 22. When the troops reached New York City on November 28, cheering crowds greeted them as they paraded up Fifth Avenue to their regimental armory, where they were formally demobilized.[25]

The return home of these units was part of the general withdrawal of National Guard forces from positions along the Mexican border that began before Labor Day in 1916 and continued through May 1917. The withdrawal occurred as U.S. political and military leaders became much less concerned about the possibility of a major conflict along the southern boundary of the United States with Mexico and much more concerned about the possibility of U.S. involvement in the war raging in Europe. In January 1917, President Wilson, increasingly preoccupied with deteriorating relations with Germany, ordered General Pershing to abandon his pursuit of Pancho Villa and begin moving his troops out of Mexico. By the beginning of the second week in February, nearly all the forces participating in the Punitive Expedition were back in the United States.[26] When Congress declared war on the Central powers on April 6, a large majority of the guardsmen who had been assigned to duty along the border had already returned home, and most of the rest followed within the next eight weeks.[27]

Private Thomas Stiff, Jr., of Troop L, First New York Cavalry, sent this crudely printed card on which he had glued a Runyon photo of himself to his fiancee, Bessie Pike, in New Jersey. He had some very good news to tell her: "Leave here the 7th of March for N.Y. All are well." Courtesy of Donald T. Stiff.

The question of whether the massive military buildup on the Mexican border in the summer of 1916 was as useless as many of the guardsmen on duty there at the time believed can be answered, at least partially. Explaining why something did not happen is often virtually impossible, and scholars cannot conclusively prove or disprove General Parker's assertion that the presence of large numbers of U.S. troops along the international boundary deterred Mexican attacks on American lives and property. Nevertheless, one suspects that the issue of why no major Mexican military attack took place on American interests after mid-1916 is far more complex than Parker claimed. Broad agreement among military historians does exist on another matter regarding the mobilization of the National Guard and its assignment to duty on the border. The deployment was useful, even crucial, because it not only helped prepare the U.S. armed forces for but hastened their entrance into the First World War. National Guard officers and regular army officers attached to Guard units gained valuable experience commanding large detachments of troops for the first time. In the process they learned to transport, train, and supply these forces. The generally good staff work of the U.S. military in France in the fall of 1917 and winter of 1918 in large part resulted from experience gained during the military buildup on the border in the summer of 1916.[28]

As thousands of pictures taken in 1916 by Robert Runyon and other photographers in towns from Brownsville to San Diego, California, amply demonstrate, the border experience enabled the War Department to experiment in the field with new equipment and modernize the U.S. armed forces to put them on a par with America's ambitions as an emerging world power. Guardsmen, who in July arrived on the Rio Grande in horse-drawn wagons carrying rifles dating from before the Spanish-American War, were by August training among armored vehicles, trucks, motorcycles, airplanes, wireless radios, heavy machine guns, and long-range artillery. Information on the performance and reliability of military hardware used for the first time by large numbers of U.S. troops during the buildup on the border was invaluable to War Department procurement specialists charged with equipping the U.S. forces sent to France.[29]

Many of the National Guard enlisted men who first learned to soldier in the heat, rain, and mud of Texas were soon called upon to apply the lessons they had learned in actual combat on the western front in France. In this respect the experience of Private Henry R. Marcoux of the Seventh New York Infantry, an imported food salesman in a Manhattan silk-stocking neighborhood when he departed for McAllen with his unit in June 1916, is typical. After coming home from the border on November 28, he and his buddies were promptly demobilized. Their return to civilian life ended when the Seventh New York Infantry was called back to active duty in July 1917 and incorporated into the Twenty-Seventh New York Division. Following a period of training in trench warfare in South Carolina, Marcoux and the other members of the division were shipped to France, assigned to the British Second Army, and began combat operations in mid-1918. The Seventh New York Infantry suffered heavy casualties during the second Somme offensive, and only fifty

General John ("Black Jack") Pershing (foreground) and General James ("Gallopin' Jim") Parker and their staffs prepare to review troops on the parade ground at Fort Brown in March 1917. Pershing had been appointed to succeed General Frederick Funston in February as commander of the Southern District of the U.S. Army following the latter's death and was on a tour of inspection of the posts in his command. Courtesy of the Barker Texas History Center.

Le Salut du Général PERSHING, Commandant en Chef des Troupes Américaines, à la terre de France (Juin 1917).

A French photographer recorded the arrival of General Pershing and his staff on French soil in June 1917, less than three months after Pershing's visit to Fort Brown. The French armed forces command issued this postcard by the thousands to its weary troops in the field to bolster their morale by showing them that help from the Americans had indeed arrived. Courtesy of Frank N. Samponaro.

of the original 250 men of Marcoux's Company M returned to the United States in 1919 without having been killed or wounded. Marcoux, who was one of the lucky ones, was discharged from the service on April 2, 1919, and returned permanently to civilian life.[30]

A picture that Robert Runyon took in March 1917 symbolized the transition then taking place in America's role in the world as well as in the responsibilities of its armed forces and the lives of many of its citizens. It showed General Pershing, who recently had returned from Mexico and been made commander of the Southern Department of the Army, and General Parker, who recently had been in charge of 28,000 troops in the Lower Rio Grande Valley, as they prepared to review Army regulars and departing National Guard troops on the parade ground at Fort Brown. By June Pershing would be in France with the first elements of the American Expeditionary Force, including some of the soldiers about to march past him. America's focus on events on the border was ending; its preoccupation with events in a wider world was beginning with enormous implications for many of the soldiers on the parade ground that day and for their families. As he had done so often in the past and would continue to do in the future, Robert Runyon was on hand with his camera to document for posterity a significant event of his times that otherwise might soon have been forgotten.

View of Fort Brown from a wireless transmission tower on the base. The horse barns are in the foreground; the white two-story building behind them on the left is the hospital. The city of Brownsville is visible in the background. Fort Brown, the oldest U.S. Army post on the Rio Grande, was established in 1846 by General Zachary Taylor and named by him after Major Jacob Brown, who died defending it on May 9, 1846. Despite having been written off by the War Department as militarily useless in 1911, Fort Brown remained open continuously from 1913 until 1945. Courtesy of the Barker Texas History Center.

A group of U.S. Army soldiers from Fort Brown on guard duty in 1916 on the railroad bridge between Brownsville and Matamoros pose with their Mexican counterparts. The bridge, which was opened in 1910 to connect the St. Louis, Brownsville and Mexico Railway with the Mexican National, remains in use today. Courtesy of the Barker Texas History Center.

ILL. CAV.
CAMP.

5

Although the headquarters of the Brownsville District was at Fort Brown, hastily constructed temporary camps for National Guard units, like this one for the First Illinois Cavalry Regiment on the outskirts of Brownsville, sprung up throughout the Lower Rio Grande Valley in the summer of 1916. Courtesy of the Barker Texas History Center.

BATTERY E. 5TH ART.
STARTING ON A
MARCH

The soldiers of Battery E, Fifth U.S. Artillery, leaving Fort Brown on a practice march. Like National Guard troops, Army regulars complained about the marches in the relentless summer heat and occasional mud of the Lower Rio Grande Valley. Courtesy of the Barker Texas History Center.

U.S. Army soldiers scaling a wall during training exercises at Fort Brown in 1914. Regular troops had been in the Lower Rio Grande Valley training strenuously, engaging in periodic firefights with Mexicans, and even getting killed for three years before the National Guard arrived en masse in 1916. Regular enlisted men did not regard the guardsmen as real soldiers and usually avoided fraternizing with them during off-duty hours. Courtesy of the Barker Texas History Center.

These Army engineers are constructing a pontoon bridge across the *resaca* (lagoon) at Fort Brown. The construction of pontoon bridges was designed to permit the rapid deployment of U.S. troops into Mexico if necessary. Courtesy of the Barker Texas History Center.

FIRST VA. INF,
IN THE TRENCHES,

Members of the First Virginia Infantry Regiment in trenches near Brownsville in the summer of 1916 aiming their Springfield rifles at an imaginary
enemy. Within eighteen months some of these men were in trenches in
France firing their weapons at German soldiers. Trench warfare, a classic
form of static combat, was not new to the U.S. military and had been
utilized by both sides during the Civil War. Courtesy of the Barker Texas
History Center.

During the summer and fall of 1916 parading troops marched frequently through the streets of Brownsville and past the reviewing stand at Fort Brown. The grandest of the parades occurred on August 9, when a column of regular Army and National Guard troops five miles long passed in review before General Parker. In this photograph members of the Virginia National Guard await inspection by General Pershing during his visit to the Lower Rio Grande Valley in March 1917. By that time most of the guardsmen had already returned home, but enough remained to help the regular Army troops of the Fort Brown garrison put on a good show for the new commanding officer of the Southern Department of the U.S. Army. Courtesy of the Barker Texas History Center.

Truck Company Number Three, Fort Brown. On his tour of inspection of Fort Brown, General Pershing had the opportunity to get a good look at some of the new equipment being used by troops stationed at the base. He already had considerable experience with motor transport. His demand for trucks to supply the Punitive Expedition in Mexico created a scramble among manufacturers anxious to obtain U.S. government contracts. In all, eight different companies supplied thirteen models of trucks to Army trans- portation units on the Mexican border in 1916 and 1917. Despite the headaches this lack of standardization of vehicles caused for motor pool supply sergeants, information on the durability and dependability of the various trucks was of great value to War Department procurement officers responsible for equipping the American Expeditionary Force in France. Courtesy of the Barker Texas History Center.

MACHINE GUN TROOP THIRD U.S. CAVALRY SHOWING VICKERS-MAXIM WATER COOLED MACHINE GUNS.

© R RUNYON.

114

Soldiers of the Third U.S. Cavalry at Fort Brown pose for Runyon with their Vickers-Maxim .30-06 caliber water-cooled machine guns. The Army liked the performance of this weapon, nicknamed by the troops the "Belgian Rattlesnake," and it became the standard heavy machine gun for U.S. troops in Europe during the First World War. Courtesy of the Barker Texas History Center.

Motorcycle troops, Fort Brown. By no means did all of the new equipment that U.S. forces used in the field for the first time on the Mexican border prove satisfactory under combat conditions. Mounting machine guns like these on motorcycles seemed to be a good idea. Experiments, however, showed that as the vehicles bounced along, machine gunners wildly and inaccurately sprayed the countryside with bullets. As a result, motorcycles, mostly Harley-Davidsons and Hendees (Indians), were soon relegated to communications work near Army and National Guard camps. Courtesy of the Barker Texas History Center.

With no enemy to fight, the guardsmen had plenty of time to pose for Runyon. He was a frequent visitor to the camps in the Brownsville area and took literally thousands of photographs like this one so the troops would have postcards to keep as souvenirs of their duty on the border and to send to the folks back home. Courtesy of the Barker Texas History Center.

Some of the boys combated their boredom by thinking of slightly unconventional ways to be photographed. Courtesy of the Barker Texas History Center.

Although far fewer in number by mid-July 1916, regular Army troops were as eager as the guardsmen to have Runyon take their picture. This real photo postcard shows two members of the Fifth U.S. Field Artillery posing with a 4.7-inch cannon. Courtesy of the Barker Texas History Center.

This young soldier may have wanted a photograph of himself to send to his parents or to his girlfriend. Courtesy of the Barker Texas History Center.

A group of soldiers at Fort Brown beside Runyon's car. A resourceful small businessman, Runyon earned some extra income selling money orders when he visited military posts to photograph the troops. Before buying this Model T Ford in 1915, Runyon used a bicycle or public transportation to travel about the Lower Rio Grande Valley. His automobile had two headlights that ran off the magneto and two acetylene parking lamps. Like other Model T Fords, Runyon's vehicle had no battery or starter; the engine was brought coughing and sputtering to life by rotating a handcrank. Runyon drove this car for twenty years until the crank kicked back one day as he tried to start it and broke his wrist. After that accident Runyon never drove again but relied on a series of chauffeurs, including his sons Robert and Delbert, to do the driving for him. Courtesy of the Barker Texas History Center.

Numerous Y.M.C.A.s were built at military posts all along the border from Texas to California during the summer of 1916. While many of the boys regarded them merely as a place to go for rest and relaxation, they were specifically intended to provide the troops with a wholesome Christian alternative to the sleazy attractions of camp and border towns. What better way was there to achieve this objective than to get the soldiers to attend Bible class? Courtesy of the Barker Texas History Center.

A few of the more athletically inclined troops joined the regimental baseball team or participated in boxing tournaments, but the enlisted men's pool at Fort Brown always drew a large crowd on hot Sunday afternoons. Courtesy of the Barker Texas History Center.

4. Military Buildup in the Lower Rio Grande Valley

1. Marcum, "Fort Brown," pp. 273, 285.

2. Coerver and Hall, *Texas and the Mexican Revolution*, pp. 64, 78, 87–91; *Brownsville Herald*, May 12, 1916; Joseph C. Sides, *Fort Brown Historical: History of Fort Brown, Texas, Border Post on the Rio Grande*, p. 143.

3. Hill, *The Minute Man in Peace and War*, pp. 230–235, 237, 242; John K. Mahon, *History of the Militia and the National Guard*, pp. 151–152; Frank Tompkins, *Chasing Villa: The Story behind the Story of Pershing's Expedition into Mexico*, p. 228.

4. Pierce, *A Brief History of the Lower Rio Grande Valley*, pp. 77–106, 155–182; Sides, *Fort Brown Historical*, pp. 143–146; *Brownsville Herald*, May 20, 1916, July 1, 1916, July 4–7, 1916, July 11–12, 1916, July 14, 1916, July 16, 1916, July 31, 1916, Aug. 9, 1916; Iowa, Adjutant General's Office, *Biennial Report of the Adjutant General of Iowa for the Biennial Period Ended November 30, 1916*, p. 45; Illinois, Adjutant General's Office, *Roster of the Illinois National Guard on the Mexican Border, 1916–1917*, p. viii; Stambaugh and Stambaugh, *The Lower Rio Grande Valley*, p. 222; Tompkins, *Chasing Villa*, p. 228.

5. Mahon, *History of the Militia and the National Guard*, p. 152; Tompkins, *Chasing Villa*, p. 229; Vanderwood and Samponaro, *Border Fury*, p. 12.

6. *Brownsville Herald*, Aug. 3, 1916.

7. Ibid., Aug. 10, 1916.

8. Illinois Adjutant General's Office, *Roster of the Illinois National Guard*, pp. viii, 577; *Brownsville Herald*, July 4, 1916, July 6, 1916.

9. *Brownsville Herald*, July 7, 1916.

10. Ibid.; see also Hill, *The Minute Man in Peace and War*, p. 237.

11. *Brownsville Herald*, July 6, 1916.

12. See Mahon, *History of the Militia and the National Guard*, p. 152.

13. Illinois, Adjutant General's Office, *Roster of the Illinois National Guard*, p. viii.

14. See ibid.; Vanderwood and Samponaro, *Border Fury*, pp. 12–13, 50–51; Tomkins, *Chasing Villa*, p. 229.

15. The only National Guard officer with a status comparable to that of O'Ryan during the military buildup on the border in the summer of 1916 was Major General James Clement, who commanded the Pennsylvania National Guard division stationed at El Paso. See Tompkins, *Chasing Villa*, p. 228.

16. *Brownsville Herald*, July 4, 1916.

17. Carl H. Marcoux, "Reminiscences of the Mexican Border, 1916," p. 1.

18. See Dewitt Clinton Falls, *History of the Seventh Regiment, 1889–1922*, pp. 166–167.

19. John B. Phillips, Jr., "Camp Life at McAllen," *Seventh Regiment Gazette* 11 (Aug. 1916): 309–310.

20. Falls, *History of the Seventh Regiment*, pp. 168–172.

21. Phillips, "Camp Life at McAllen," pp. 311–313, 316.

22. Ibid., p. 318.

23. Ibid., p. 312.

24. *Brownsville Herald*, Aug. 30–31, 1916.

25. Falls, *History of the Seventh Regiment*, pp. 178–179.

26. Leon C. Metz, *Fort Bliss: An Illustrated History*, p. 74.

27. Hill, *The Minute Man in Peace and War*, p. 242.

28. Tompkins, *Chasing Villa*, p. 229; Mahon, *History of the Militia and the National Guard*, p. 152.

29. Vanderwood and Samponaro, *Border Fury*, pp. 179–260.

30. Marcoux, "Reminiscences of the Mexican Border, 1916," p. 2; Falls, *History of The Seventh Regiment*, pp. 180–182.

Appendix A

Inventory of Robert Runyon's Photo Studio, January 1, 1922

PICTURE FRAMES AND MOULDING

22	11 x 14 Framed Photographs		44.00	15	6 x 8 Framed Photographs	7.50
28	8 x 10 Framed Photographs		18.00	7	Panoramas 2.00 ea	14.00
5	5 x 12 Framed Photographs	.50 ea	2.50		Assortment of picture moulding	70.00

EQUIPMENT AND OTHER MATERIAL

1	Book Case and desk	35.00
1	Iron Safe	125.00
1	Victor Flash Cabinet	150.00

CAMERAS

2	5 x 7 Korona View Cameras 38.00	76.00
1	Korona Home Portrait Camera	36.00
1	Korona Panoramic View Camera, 5 x 12	50.00
1	Korona Folding Studio Stand	14.00
1	Korona Enlarging Attachment, 8 x 10	8.00
2	Korona Reducing Backs, 3 ¼ x 5 ½	14.00
1	No. 1, Combination Korona Tripod	5.00
1	No. 1, Century Camera with Focal plane shutter, level and finder	70.00
1	Korona View Camera, size 8 x 10	45.00
1	Graphic Enlarging Camera	30.00
1	Lantern Slide Camera	35.00
1	No. 7 Century Studio Camera	40.00
1	Cirkut Camera No. 10 and outfit	320.00
1	Seneca View Camera, 8 x 10	35.00
1	Sanderson Tropical Hand and Stand Camera Extra Quality Sole Leather Case and 3 Book Form Slides and 10 plate Holders, Made of Teak	100.00
1	Picture Frame Vise	6.00
1	Mitre and Saw	11.00

PRINTING MATERIAL

2 Cuts	.30 cents ea.	6.60
5 "	.85 cents ea.	4.25
5 "	1.10 ea.	5.50
1 "	.50	.50
3 Cuts	.25 cents ea.	.75

1	5 x 8 Excelsior Printing press		35.00
1	Hardwood Cabinet for type, etc.		20.00
8	Type Cases	2.25 each	18.00
1	Font No. 610 type		1.20
2	Fonts 609 type	1.20 each	2.40
2	Fonts 628 type	1.45	2.90
1	Font 638		3.00
1	Font. No. 737 type		2.50
2	Fonts No. 630 type	2.50 ea.	5.00
2	Fonts No. 727	1.75 ea.	3.50
2	Pounds 8 point leaders		.80
1	Font Labor saving Brass Rule		4.00
1	Font Labor saving metal furniture		4.50
1	Font No. 23 Border		1.40
1	Font No. 43 Border		1.40
	Misc. items: Brass rule, Extra Quads, Wooden Furniture Dashes, etc.		2.50

STUDIO FURNITURE

1	Posing Chair	6.00
4	Chairs at $3.00 ea.	12.00
2	Stand Tables at $5.00 ea.	10.00
1	Mirror	15.00
1	Posing bench	5.00
1	Show case	5.00
1	Wooden Post card rack	5.00
2	Revolving metal post card racks $2.50 ea.	5.00
2	Kitchen Tables, $2.50 ea.	5.00
1	Background carrier, 10 x 12 ft.	10.00
1	Reflector carrier	5.00
		1,679.70

Source: Inventory, Robert Runyon, Photographer, Brownsville,Tex., Jan. 1, 1922, Robert Runyon Document File, Barker Texas History Center, University of Texas at Austin.

Appendix B

Plan de San Diego

PLAN (PLOT) OF SAN DIEGO, STATE OF TEXAS, JANUARY 6TH, 1915

We who in turn sign our names, assembled in the REVOLUTIONARY PLOT OF SAN DIEGO, TEXAS, solemnly promise each other, on our word of honor, that we will fulfill, and cause to be fulfilled and complied with, all the clauses and provisions stipulated in this document, and execute the orders and wishes emanating from the PROVISIONAL DIRECTORATE of this movement, and recognize as military Chief of the same, Mr. Augustin [*sic*] S. GARZA, guaranteeing with our lives the faithful accomplishment of what is here agreed upon.

1. On the 20th day of February, 1915, at two o'clock in the morning, we will arise in arms against the Government and Country of the United States of North America, ONE AS ALL AND ALL AS ONE, proclaiming the liberty of individuals of the black race and its independence of Yankee tyranny which has held us in iniquitous slavery since remote times; and at the same time and in the same manner we will proclaim the independence and segregation of the States bordering upon the Mexican Nation, which are: TEXAS, NEW MEXICO, ARIZONA, COLORADO, and UPPER CALIFORNIA, of which States the REPUBLIC OF MEXICO was robbed in a most perfidious manner by North American imperialism.

2. In order to render the foregoing clause effective, the necessary army corps will be formed, under the immediate command of military leaders named by the SUPREME REVOLUTIONARY CONGRESS of SAN DIEGO, TEXAS, which shall have full power to designate a SUPREME CHIEF, who shall be at the head of said army. The banner which shall guide us in this enterprise shall be red, with a white diagonal fringe, and bearing the following inscription: "EQUALITY AND INDEPENDENCE" and none of the subordinate leaders or subalterns shall use any other flag (except only the white flag for signals). The aforesaid army shall be known by the name of: "LIBERATING ARMY FOR RACES AND PEOPLES."

3. Each one of the chiefs will do his utmost, by whatever means possible, to get possession of arms and funds of the cities which he has beforehand been designated to capture, in order that our cause may be provided with resources to continue the fight with better success, the said leaders each being required to render an account of everything to his superiors, in order that the latter may dispose of it in the proper manner.

4. The leader who may take a city must immediately name and appoint municipal authorities, in order that they may preserve order and assist in every way possible the revolutionary movement. In case the Capital of any State which we are endeavoring to liberate be captured, there will be named in the same manner superior municipal authorities, for the same purpose.

5. It is strictly forbidden to hold prisoners, either special prisoners (civilians) or soldiers; and the only time that should be spent in dealing with them is that which is absolutely necessary to demand funds (loans) of them; and whether these demands be successful or not, they shall be shot immediately, without any pretext.

6. Every stranger who shall be found armed and who cannot prove his right to carry arms, shall be summarily executed, regardless of his race or nationality.

7. Every North American over sixteen years of age shall be put to death; and only the aged men, the women, and the children shall be respected; and on no account shall the traitors to our race be respected.

8. The APACHES of Arizona, as well as the INDIANS (Redskins) of the territory, shall be given every guarantee; and their lands which have been taken from them shall be returned to them, to the end that they may assist us in the cause which we defend.

9. All appointments and grades in our army which are exercised by subordinate officers (subalterns) shall be examined (recognized) by the superior officers. There shall likewise be recognized the grades of the leaders of other complots which may not be connected with this, and who may wish to co-operate with us; also those who may affiliate with us later.

10. The movement having gathered force, and once having possessed ourselves of the States above alluded to, we shall proclaim them an INDE-PENDENT REPUBLIC, later requesting (if it be thought expedient) annexation to MEXICO, without concerning ourselves at that time about the form of government which may control the destinies of the common mother country.

11. When we shall have obtained independence for the negroes, we shall grant them a banner, which they themselves shall be permitted to select, and we shall aid them in obtaining six States of the American Union, which States border upon those already mentioned, and they may form these six States a republic, and they may be, therefore, independent.

12. None of the leaders shall have power to make terms with the enemy, without first communicating with the superior officers of the army, bearing in mind that this is a war without quarter; nor shall any leader enroll in his ranks any stranger, unless said stranger belong to the Latin, the Negro, or the Japanese race.

13. It is understood that none of the members of this COMPLOT (or any one who may come in later), shall, upon the definite triumph of the cause which we defend, fail to recognize their superiors, nor shall the said others who, with bastard designs, may endeavor to destroy what has been accomplished by such great work.

14. As soon as possible, each local society (junta) shall nominate delegates who shall meet at a time and place before hand designated, for the purpose of nominating a PERMANENT DIRECTORATE OF THE REVOLUTIONARY MOVEMENT. At this meeting shall be determined and worked out in detail the powers and duties of the PERMANENT DIRECTORATE, and this REV-OLUTIONARY PLAN may be revised or amended.

15. It is understood among those who may follow this movement that we will carry as a signing voice the independence of the negroes, placing obligations upon both races; and that, on no account will we accept aid, either moral or pecuniary, from the Government of Mexico; and it need not consider itself under any obligations in this, our movement.

"EQUALITY AND INDEPENDENCE."

San Diego, Texas, Jan. 6, 1915.

Secretary

(Signed) A. Gonzales, lawyer

PRESIDENT.

(Signed) L. Ferringo.

Augustin S. Garza	(Signed) A. S. Garza, Commisionman [sic].
(Signed) Manuel Flores.	(Signed) A. A. Saenz, Saloon keeper.
(Signed) B. Ramos Jr.	(Signed) E. Cisneros.
(Signed) A. C. Almaraz.	(Signed) Porfirio Santos.

I certify that the foregoing is a correct translation of the document marked "Exhibit 1."

_____
Immigrant Inspector.

[Source: Webb (Walter Prescott) Papers, File 2R290, Texas Ranger Correspondence, Adjutant General's Office. Barker Texas History Center, University of Texas at Austin. The Spanish original is not in this file. The translator is unknown.]

Selected Bibliography

BOOKS

Allhands, J. L. *Gringo Builders*. N.p., 1931.

Brownsville High School. *Palmetto*. Brownsville: Brownsville High School, 1918–1925.

Canesco Botello, José Raul. *Historia de Matamoros*. 2nd ed. Matamoros, Tamaulipas, Mexico: Talleres Tipográficos de Litografía Jardín, 1981.

Casey, Robert J. *The Texas Border*. New York: Bobbs Merrill Company, Inc., 1950.

Chatfield, W. H., ed. *Twin Cities of the Border—Brownsville, Texas and Matamoros, Mexico—and the Country of the Lower Rio Grande*. New Orleans: E. P. Brandao, 1893.

Clendenen, Clarence C. *The United States and Pancho Villa: A Study in Unconventional Diplomacy*. Port Arthur, N.Y.: Kennikat Press, 1961.

Coerver, Don M., and Linda B. Hall. *Texas and the Mexican Revolution: A Study in State and National Border Policy, 1910–1920*. San Antonio: Trinity University Press, 1984.

Derthick, Martha. *The National Guard in Politics*. Cambridge, Mass.: Harvard University Press, 1965.

Devlin, Thomas F. *Days of Discord: A Brief Chronology of the Mexican Revolution, 1910–1920*. El Paso: American Printing Company, 1974.

Dupuy, R. Ernest. *The National Guard: A Compact History*. New York: Hawthorn Books, Inc., 1971.

Facts about Brownsville, Texas. San Antonio: Rawson and Company, Inc., 1968.

Falls, Dewitt Clinton. *History of the Seventh Regiment, 1899–1922*. New York: Veterans of the Seventh Regiment, 1948.

Ferguson, Henry. *The Port of Brownsville: A Maritime History of the Lower Rio Grande Valley*. Brownsville: Spring-King Press, 1976.

Fleischauer, Carl, and Beverly W. Brannan. *Documenting America, 1935–1943*. Berkeley: University of California Press, 1988.

Garza Treviño, Ciro R. de la. *La revolución mexicana en el Estado de Tamaulipas*. Mexico City: Librería de Manuel Porrúa, n.d.

Gilbert, Minnie. *Roots by the River: A Story of Texas Tropical Borderland Valley By-Liners*. Book 2. Ed. Teresa Chapa Alamía, and Elena Farías Barrera. Mission: Border Kingdom Press, 1978.

Gilderhus, Mark T. *Diplomacy and Revolution: U.S.-Mexican Relations Under Wilson and Carranza*. Tucson: University of Arizona Press, 1977.

Gutierrez de Lara, L., and Edcumb Pinchon. *The Mexican People: Their Struggle for Freedom*. Garden City, N.Y.: Doubleday, Page and Company, 1914.

Hall, Linda B., and Don M. Coerver. *Revolution and the Border: The United States and Mexico, 1910–1920*. Albuquerque: University of New Mexico Press, 1988.

Hart, John Mason. *Revolutionary Mexico: The Coming and Process of the Mexican Revolution*. Berkeley: University of California Press, 1987.

Hill, Jim Dan. *The Minute Man in Peace and War: A History of the National Guard*. Harrisburg, Pa.: Stackpole Company, 1964.

Holt, Tonie, and Valmai Holt. *Till the Boys Come Home: The Picture Postcards of the First World War*. Newtown Square, Pa.: Deltiologists of America, 1977.

Illinois. Adjutant General's Office. *Roster of the Illinois National Guard on the Mexican Border, 1916–1917*. Springfield: State of Illinois, 1928.

Iowa. Adjutant General's Office. *Biennial Report of the Adjutant General of Iowa for the Biennial Period Ended November 30, 1916*. Des Moines: State of Iowa, 1916.

Kearney, Milo, ed. *Studies in Brownsville History*. Brownsville: Pan American University at Brownsville, 1986.

Knight, Alan. *The Mexican Revolution*. 2 vols. Cambridge, England: Cambridge University Press, 1988.

Mahon, John K. *History of the Militia and the National Guard*. New York: Macmillan Publishing Company, 1983.

María y Campos, Armando de. *La Vida del General Lucio Blanco*. Mexico City: Talleres Gráficos de la Nación, 1963.

Maril, Robert Lee. *Poorest of Americans: The Mexican-Americans of the Lower Rio Grande Valley of Texas*. South Bend: University of Notre Dame Press, 1989.

Martínez, Oscar J. *Fragments of the Mexican Revolution: Personal Accounts from the Border*. Albuquerque: University of New Mexico Press, 1983.

Metz, Leon C. *Border: The U.S.–Mexico Line*. El Paso: Mangan Books, 1989.

———. *Fort Bliss: An Illustrated History*. El Paso: Mangan Books, 1981.

Montejano, David. *Anglos and Mexicans in the Making of Texas*. Austin: University of Texas Press, 1987.

Morgan, Hal, and Andreas Brown. *Prairie Fires and Paper Moons: The American Photographic Postcard, 1900–1920*. Boston: David R. Godine, 1981.

Pierce, Frank C. *A Brief History of the Lower Rio Grande Valley.* Menasha, Wis.: George Banta Publishing Company, 1917.

Pope, Dorothy Lee. *Rainbow Era on the Rio Grande.* Brownsville: Springman-King Company, 1971.

Putnam, George Haven. *The Question of Copyright.* New York: G. P. Putnam's Sons, 1896.

Rayburn, John C., and Virginia Kemp Rayburn, eds. *Century of Conflict: Incidents in the Lives of William Neale and William A. Neale, Early Settlers in Texas.* Waco: Texian Press, 1966.

Robertson, Brian. *Rio Grande Heritage: A Pictorial History.* Norfolk, Va.: The Donning Company Publishers, 1985.

Runyon, Robert. *Genealogy of the Descendants of Anthony Lawson of Northumberland England.* Brownsville: By the Author, 808 Saint Charles Street, 1952.

―――. *Mirror Plater's Guide.* Catlettsburg, Ky.: By the Author, n.d.

―――. *Supplement to Runyon Genealogy.* Harlingen: United Printers and Publishers, 1962.

―――. *Vernacular Names of Plants Indigenous to the Lower Rio Grande Valley.* Brownsville: By the Author, 808 Saint Charles Street, 1947.

Runyon, Robert, and Amos Runyon. *Runyon Genealogy.* Brownsville: By the Authors, 808 Saint Charles Street, 1955.

Ryan, Dorothy B. *Picture Postcards in the United States, 1893–1918.* 1st ed., rev. New York: Clarkson N. Potter, 1986.

Samora, Julian, Joe Bernal, and Albert Peña. *Gunpowder Justice: A Reassessment of the Texas Rangers.* South Bend: University of Notre Dame Press, 1979.

Schulz, Ellen D., and Robert Runyon. *Texas Cacti: A Popular and Scientific Account of the Cacti Native of Texas.* San Antonio: Texas Academy of Science, 1930.

ARTICLES

Anders, Evan. "Boss Rule and Constituent Interests: South Texas Politics During the Progressive Era." *Southwestern Historical Quarterly* 74 (Jan. 1981): 269–292.

Conniff, Richard. "When 'Fiends' Pressed the Button, There Was No Place to Hide." *Smithsonian* 19 (June 1988): 106–117.

Cumberland, Charles C. "Border Raids in the Lower Rio Grande Valley, 1915." *Southwestern Historical Quarterly* 57 (Jan. 1954): 285–311.

Gerlach, Allen. "Conditions along the Border—1915: The Plan of San Diego." *New Mexico Historical Review* 43 (July 1958): 195–212.

Hager, William A. "The Plan of San Diego: Unrest on the Texas Border in 1915." *Arizona and the West* 5 (Winter 1963): 327–336.

Harris, Charles H. III, and Louis R. Sadler, "The Plan of San Diego and the Mexican-United States War Crisis of 1916: A Reexamination." In *The Border and the Revolution*, pp. 71–98. Las Cruces: Center for Latin American Studies/Joint Border Research Institute, New Mexico State University, 1988.

Ideker, Joe. "Robert Runyon, Pioneer Lower Rio Grande Valley Botanist." *Sabal* 5 (Dec. 1988): 1–5.

O'Donnell, Dick. "Cards: Post of the Town." *San Antonio Express-News*, May 3, 1987.

Phillips, John B., Jr. "Camp Life at McAllen." *Seventh Regiment Gazette* 11 (Aug. 1916): 309–310.

Quiñones, Juan Gómez. "The Plan of San Diego Renewed." *Aztlán* 1 (Spring 1970): 124–132.

Richmond, Douglas W. *"La guerra de Texas se renova;* Mexican Insurrection and Carrancista Ambitions, 1900–1920." *Aztlán* 11 (Spring 1980): 1–32.

Rocha, Rodolfo. "Banditry in the Lower Rio Grande Valley of Texas, 1915." *Studies in History* 6 (1976): 55–73.

Sandos, James A. "The Plan de San Diego: War and Diplomacy on the Texas Border, 1915–1916." *Arizona and the West* 14 (Spring 1972): 5–24.

Vanderwood, Paul J. "The Picture Postcard as Historical Evidence: Veracruz, 1914." *The Americas* 45 (Oct. 1988): 201–226.

―――. "Writing History with Picture Postcards: Revolution in Tijuana." *Journal of San Diego History* 34 (Winter 1988): 38–63.

Watts, Jake. "The Plan of San Diego and the Lower Rio Grande Valley." In *More Studies in Brownsville History.* Ed. Milo Kearney, pp. 322–345. Brownsville: Pan American University at Brownsville, 1989.

UNPUBLISHED DOCUMENTS

Cameron County Clerk's Office. Vault, Record of Alien Ownership, vol. 1. Brownsville.

Curt Teich and Company. "Geographic Index for Brownsville, Texas, 1911–1940." Curt Teich Postcard Collection, Lake County Museum, Wauconda, Ill.

McClung, John Busby. "The Rangers along the Rio Grande, 1910–1919." Master's thesis, Texas Christian University, 1963.

Mahoney, Lillian R. Interview. Austin. Oct. 20, 1989.

Marcoux, Carl H. "Reminiscences of the Mexican Border, 1916." Newport Beach, Calif., 1989.

Marcum, Richard. "Fort Brown, Texas: The History of a Border Post." Ph.D. diss., Texas Tech University, 1964.

Perkins, Amali R. Interview. San Antonio. Sept. 24, 1988.

Perkins, Douglas. "Robert Runyon Biographical Sketch." Robert Runyon Document File, Barker Texas History Center, University of Texas at Austin.

Robert Runyon Document File. Barker Texas History Center. University of Texas at Austin.

Rocha, Rodolfo. "The Influence of the Mexican Revolution on the Mexico-Texas Border, 1910–1916." Ph.D. diss., Texas Tech University, 1981.

Runyon, Delbert. Interviews. Brownsville. Oct. 22, 1988, and July 28, 1989.

Runyon Family. Interviews with various Runyon family members. Runyon Family Reunion. Austin. Oct. 20, 1989.

Runyon, Robert. "Report Made by Robert Runyon to the Citizens of Brownsville at a Public Meeting Held in the Cameron County Courthouse." June 20, 1940. Robert Runyon Document File, Barker Texas History Center, University of Texas at Austin.

[Runyon, Robert.] "History, Data, and Information Relative to Robert Runyon, P. O. Box 11, Brownsville, Texas." N.p., n.d. Robert Runyon Document File, Barker Texas History Center, University of Texas at Austin.

Runyon, Robert A. Interview. Brownsville. July 28, 1989.

Sandos, James A. "The Mexican Revolution and the United States, 1915–1917: The Impact of Conflict in the Tamaulipas-Texas Frontier upon the Emergence of Revolutionary Governments in Mexico." Ph.D. diss., University of California, Berkeley, 1978.

Sapia-Bosch, Alfonso F. "The Role of Lucio Blanco in the Mexican Revolution, 1913–1922." Ph.D. diss., Georgetown University, 1977.

Southwest Medical Society. "Program of the Fifth and Sixth Districts, Southwest Medical Society Meeting, El Jardin Hotel, Brownsville, Texas, July 2 and 3, 1916." Robert Runyon Document File, Barker Texas History Center, University of Texas at Austin.

Stiff, Donald T. Interview. Orlando, Fla. Dec. 2, 1989.

U.S. National Archives, Southwestern Region, Record Group 21, Records of the United States District Courts, Southern District of Texas, Brownsville, N. 552 at law.

Webb (Walter Prescott) Papers, File 2R290. Barker Texas History Center. University of Texas at Austin.

NEWSPAPERS and MAGAZINES

Brownsville Herald. 1910–1943, 1950, 1968, 1983.

Catlettsburg *Tribune.* 1910.

Houston Chronicle. 1921.

Houston Post. 1913–1916, 1921, 1923, 1926.

Monty's Monthly Digest of Valley Activities. 1919–1920, 1927.

Rio Grande Valley: Herald of Progress: A Picture Journey through the Rio Grande Valley of Texas. 1923.

San Antonio Evening News. 1947.

San Antonio Express. 1913.

San Antonio Light. 1913–1916.

Seventh Regiment Gazette. 1916.

Texas Commercial News. 1924.

Valley Morning Star. 1952.

Index

Page numbers in *italics* refer to photographs.

Designed and printed at Wind River Press

DUE DATE

Printed
in USA